Employment Problems
under the Conditions of Rapid Technological Change

D1721489

Schriften zu Regional- und Verkehrsproblemen
in Industrie- und Entwicklungsländern

Herausgegeben von J. Heinz Müller und Theodor Dams

Band 46

Editors' Foreword

The Economics Faculties of Freiburg University, Fed. Rep. of Germany, and of Nagoya University, Japan, submit in this publication the papers presented and discussed at the VIII Joint Seminar (spring 1984 in Freiburg). The overall theme „Employment Problems under the Conditions of Rapid Technological Change" was dealt with in 15 different papers; we do hope that they cover the broad spectrum of this critical issue, which has become one of the great scientific challenges of today. For the first time, contributions to the joint seminar are published in English in order to bring attention to the research and results of the cooperation between Freiburg and Nagoya within a broader international scientific community.

The cooperation between Freiburg and Nagoya is presently in its 10th year; in October 1986, on the occasion of the X Joint Seminar in Freiburg, the documents of the Agreement of Scientific Cooperation were officially exchanged. The agreement covers the following main areas:

1. Scientific cooperation in research
2. Organization of joint seminars
3. Mutual support in teaching and research
4. Exchange of researchers
5. Exchange of graduate students
6. Exchange of scientific publications and information.

In the meantime, cooperation is carried out on different levels: The yearly seminars, which are held alternately in Nagoya and Freiburg, offer opportunities for the exchange of scientific experiences. The arrangement of visiting professorships opens up opportunities for long-term research activities in each host country. The exchange of graduate and doctoral students, as well as their supervision and financial support, lead to a joint responsibility for the younger scientific generation.

Out of this threefold approach — seminars, visiting professorships, and exchange of doctoral students — has resulted a mutually bonded and strong network of fruitful scientific cooperation, which has lasted over 10 years.

The publishers are grateful to the chairman of the Japanese work group, Prof. Dr. Masaichi Mizuno, and to Prof. Dr. Takashi Matsugi for their openness in the collaboration, which is also apparent in the submitted publication. Our thanks also go to the "Wissenschaftliche Gesellschaft in Freiburg i. Br." and to the "Verband der Freunde der Universität Freiburg e.V." for their support of this publication.

The editorial responsibility for this publication was assumed by Mr. H. J. Laabs; technical work was executed by the secretariat of the Institute for Development Policy (IFEP) of Freiburg University.

Theodor Dams   *J. Heinz Müller*

Table of Contents

Employment Policy by Shortening Working Hours

Alois Oberhauser

Stephan Joß

Introduction

In the Federal Republic of Germany a fierce dispute has flared up as to whether unemployment can be reduced by shortening working hours. The transition to a 35-hour work-week is demanded by a great part of the trade unions. This reduction in working hours has to be combined with full wage compensation in order to avoid a fall in the standard of living for the employees and a drop in demand for consumer goods at the same time.

Some of the trade unions do not propose lowering the number of hours worked weekly, but rather reducing the number of years spent working in a lifetime. The federal government has tried to support this method of shortening the amount of time worked as well, passing regulations that make an earlier transition to retirement easier (regulation of pre-retirement).

Above all, employers fear that a reduction in working hours will lead to higher costs for the enterprises - at least if it is combined with full wage compensation. This would spur price increases, which would aggravate the economic situation, preventing an improvement in the situation on the labor market. In fact, it might even result in still higher unemployment. Therefore, the employers have already rejected the introduction of a 35-hour work-week. However, they are showing less opposition to a temporary lowering of the retirement age, if the government is willing to a large part of the ensuing costs, or if it is counterbalanced by lower wage increases.

The discussion on shortening working hours is very emotionally charged, and it is the task of science to help make this discussion more objective. This is possible by the arguments towards the real economic effects and conditions, and by including economic growth in the examination.

Macroeconomic Effects

A reduction in the number of hours worked weekly has been taking place more or less continuously over the last hundred years. The weekly working hours declined from approximately 70 hours in the last century to 40 hours - which seems to represent a magic limit today. At the same time the number of hours worked yearly has also decreased, due to longer vacations. Furthermore, working-life has been shortened by lowering the retirement age limit and by extending the length of time spent in education. Parallel to these developments, considerable increases in real income took place over the last decades, and, especially since World War II, high rates of growth in the national product. If shortening working hours is regarded as one aspect of growth, the growth rate was much higher in reality than is revealed in the rise in the national product.

As long as productivity continues to rise, it is unreasonable to limit the process of shortening working hours to merely 40 hours per week. Herein lies the weakness of the employers' position. The question is not whether average working hours decrease, but the rapidity and manner in which this decrease takes place.

With regards to the macroeconomic employment effects, there are no fundamental differences between the various forms of shortening working hours. Through the measures mentioned, an attempt is made to distribute the existing

jobs among a greater number of employees. In the following, only the reduction in average weekly working hours
will be discussed, both for reasons of simplification and
because the public discussion concentrates on this
aspect.

It is necessary to start with the explanation of the real
economic basic relations to determine the macroeconomic
effects of a reduction in working hours. The basis of the
following comments is the fact that real income always
arises in direct proportion to goods and services which
are produced - taking capital depreciation into account.
Therefore, the total real income is the same as the value
of total production, which is the national product. Only
those goods are consumed which are offered on the
domestic market. Obviously, in the case of a constant
rate of savings for those persons employed, the development of the real wage basically depends on the change in
the quantity of domestic available consumer goods. The
volume of consumer goods does not develop entirely
parallel to the national product due to changes in the
investment ratio, changes in the government share in
distribution and changes in the proportion of exports and
imports in goods and services. However, the structure of
use of the national product shall be assumed to remain
constant in the following.

With that, the scope for real wage increases results from
the average growth in production per worker or per
working hour (=productivity progress), in view of the
modifications mentioned. The improvement in productivity
can be used totally or partly in reducing working hours.
A potential increase in production and with it a rise in
real wages will be foregone according to the amount in
which work-hours are decreased. Shortened working hours
must always be judged in respect to advances in
productivity. Therefore, two ways of shortening working
hours can be distinguished:

- Shortening working hours within the framework of an advance in productivity
- shortening working hours beyond the increase in productivity.

It is difficult to estimate the manner in which productivity per working hour will develop in the future, because of the very different gains in productivity in the various sectors. New technologies are causing considerable increases in productivity, especially through the use of robots, modern communication, and computers in single sectors such as the car industry, or is to some extent in the service industries. But at the same time, the realisation of that technological progress is spread over longer introductory periods. There are also sectors with relatively low productivity growth. On the whole, advances in productivity will be lower in the future than in the fifties or sixties. The high increases of those years were in particular due to knowledge which existed abroad and which could be drawn upon.

Shortening Working Hours within the Limits of an Increase in Productivity

The examination of the real-economic aspect reveals that under a given structure of use of the national product, the real wages (hourly wages) are able to rise in accordance with increases in productivity. If, on the other hand, the productivity advance is used entirely for shortening working hours and not for expanding production, the real income will be able to remain at the same level despite fewer working hours, in which case the employees produce the same quantity of goods as they did before. A real increase in their income is in fact impossible. In the case of shortened working hours, a wage compensation results from the particular use of the improvement in productivity.

Thus, if the advance in productivity is used totally for shortening working hours, the average real income is not able to increase due to the lack of additional goods. It is impossible to make use of the advance in productivity twice. It is available only once, either for a real wage increase or for shortening working hours (or a combination of both).

This will be clarified through the following example: If the increase in productivity is assumed to be 3 percent yearly, the number of working hours per week will be able to drop a little bit more than one hour each year on the average. If the employees totally forego a real income increase, the 35-hour work-week could be achieved in this way for those persons already employed in about four years, though their real income remains constant. However, a combination of shortened working hours and real wage increases might be more realistic and more in line with the needs of the employees. If an average productivity increase of 3 percent is taken as a basis, the weekly working hours will be able to decrease by one half hour per year. And at the same time, the average income can increase by 1,5 percent. This possibility is available if the increase in productivity is used half for real wage increases and half for shortening working hours.

Consequently, the hourly wages will increase by about 3 percent, production by about 1,5 percent. Transferring this example to reality - appart from the possible changes in the structure of use of the national product - advances in productivity which are themselves induced by shortening working hours must also be taken into consideration. These advances in productivity can result above all from an increased willingness and ability of the workers, which is brought about by shorter working hours. These advances can enlarge the amount of real wage increase and enable a further reduction in working hours.

Every increase in productivity leads to redundancy effects if looked at it in isolation. In the past, these redundancy effects were counterbalanced by greater production and shortened working hours. Today, reduced working hours might be helpful to prevent redundancy effects. Shortened working hours as well as real wage increases are suitable to prevent a further increase in unemployment, if they remain within the real-economic framework. Assuming 3 percent yearly productivity growth 750.000 employees could continue to work, who would otherwise become redundant under stagnating production. The first type of shortened working hours is not able to reduce existing unemployment. Because of that, the existing growth potential in the form of unemployed workers can not be drawn upon. Unemployment could only be decreased by expanding demand in a way which is neutral according to effects on the cost niveau, or expanding production. By itself, the first method of shortening working hours does not result in lowered unemployment.

Shortening Working Hours by an Amount Exceeding the Increase in Productivity

Therefore the question exists whether a decrease in working hours exceeding the increase in productivity would be able to create new jobs. Assuming a given level of production, shortened working hours exceeding improvements in productivity, would mean that further employees have to be hired on, whereby unemployment would decrease. The lack of demand for work would be distributed among more persons. It must be taken into account, however, that an increase in productivity could arise from the shortening of working hours. This reduces the need for further workers. For an individual firm, structural adjustment problems arise. But experience with reduced working hours in the past shows that the adjustment elasticity of the economy is quite large. The opposing arguments which have been expressed in many forms are mostly exaggerated.

However, at a given level of production, the total real income is the same as it was before. The real income of the other employees will inevitably decrease, because the previously unemployed workers are now receiving income. Their income does not, however, necessarily have to decrease to the same amount of the income received by unemployed previously. They already absorbed one part of the volume of consumer goods before, because they were receiving unemployment benefits. If the government does not use the decrease in unemployment benefit payments to buy goods and services, but instead uses it to reduce the burden on the private sector, then the income of those persons who have always been employed must sink by an amount equal to the difference between the income of the previously unemployed and the unemployment benefits which were granted to them. Therefore, a full wage compensation is impossible in a real-economical view.

These conclusions are only valid under certain conditions. First of all, it is assumed that the structure of use of the national product does not change by the shortening of working hours. For example, it is just as possible that private investment will rise to create further jobs. These are necessary to satisfy the total demand for goods, which is assumed to be constant. However, this is hardly to be reckoned with, due to the less than full utilization of capacity in nearly all sectors of the economy.

A further problem results from the fact that the real national product must not decrease. In this case, the positive employment effects of reduced working hours would more or less be destroyed. If either the fall in demand or the price increases resulting from a rise in costs lead to a restrictive monetary or fiscal policy, a drop in the national product can be expected. A decrease in demand can be prevented if the shortening of working hours is carried out gradually and at different times for various firms within a single industry. The reductions in working hours in the past which we mentioned above have produced almost no negative demand or employment effects. The actual problem is the rise in the unit costs. Even with the first method of shortening working hours it is to be expected that the trade unions will not abstain from further demands for wage increases, which will lack any equivalent in goods. The second method of shortening working hours, which is based on the first, would even require that the trade unions refrain from full wage compensation. That means, that they will have to accept a (temporary) decrease in real wages. Such wage behaviour by the trade unions is hardly to be expected. Ignoring the real-economic relations, the trade unions will probably push through nominal wage increases that will not be met by increases in consumer goods. They generally refer to previous or expected price increases or call upon the wrong buying power argument to defend their demands.

Not only the danger of cost-push inflation arises from such nominal wage increases, but also the danger of an intensification of the still existing stagflation. This is the well known process whereby a rise in unit costs, which is induced by a wage increase, always leads to further price increases. Therefore, monetary and fiscal policy attempt to counteract that price increase with restrictive measures and thus lead to increasing unemployment. These correlations will not be gone into in more detail. These are the most unfavorable employment effects caused by shortening working hours.

Summary

Due to the difficulties involved with raising employment through an expansion in production, it seems reasonable to use one part of the productivity advances for a gradual shortening of working hours. This must be taken into account when wage increases are being considered. If the entire increase in productivity is used for a reduction of working hours, there will, in fact, be no room left for wage increases. The only benefit is having avoided further redundancy effects, a reduction in unemployment cannot be attained.

An additional reduction in working hours exceeding the increase in productivity, (shortening working hours by the second method) will only be promising if demands for full wage compensation are given up. Otherwise, the danger exists that stagflation will increase, and that in the final result, unemployment is more likely to rise.

Productivity, Employment and Turnover in Japanese Manufacturing Industries

Kuramitsu Muramatsu

I Introduction

It has been commonly thought that rapid technological changes such as the "first industrial revolution" or in recent times, the "micro-electronics revolution" might lead to increased unemployment. But this claim is obscure theoretically and also empirically. Theoretically, it is not certain that technological changes lead to general reductions in the demand for labor. While they lead directly to a saving of labor due to higher productivity with given fixed output, they could also stimulate new investments and more consumption, and hence bring about higher aggregate demand. Even on the level of a specific industry, the effect of technological changes on employment is not certain, since there are two offsetting effects on employment. The first effect is to save labor, the second effect is to increase the demand for goods by reducing production costs, an effect dependent on the elasticity of the demand for each product with regard to its price.

It seems likely, however, that changing technology has eliminated many old jobs and created new jobs both outside of the directly affected firms as well as within them. In the process of changing jobs, some workers might experience unemployment because it takes time for dislocated workers to be matched to new jobs. Increasingly rapid shifts in skill requirements cause an increase in "structural" or "technological" unemployment. This is one of the main theoretical routes by which technological changes are connected with unemployment. But, it is empirically difficult to distinguish technological unemployment from other types of unemployment. In spite of this, one can observe that workers dismissed for economic reasons in "declining" industries tend to suffer from long-term unemployment. The number of dismissals will be one of the main points dealt with in this paper concerning technological unemployment.

In Japan, although the total rate of unemployment has increased from one percent to around 2.5 percent between 1970 and 1983, the level and also the extent of this upward trend were still lower than those in western countries. One of the reasons for lower unemployment frequently cited is the "Japanese employment practice", in which firms make an effort to avoid dismissals as far as possible by utilizing other measures such as flexible working hours, restrictions on recruitment, temporary workers and transfers within firms or to other related firms. To what extent are these practices effective? Or, are these practices unique in Japan? By estimating employment functions, international comparrisons of the adjustment speed of employment and the responsiveness of adjustment to output changes have been made in some of the relevant literature.[1] These authors have ascertained that employment tends to react slower to changes in output in Japan than in the U.S., but not so different from that in West Germany and the U.K.. These investigations have some merits, but they do not deal directly with the possibility of dismissal but with the rate of turnover of employees. Also, their main objective is to examine the short-run impact of recessions on employment. In the medium term, the capacity for internal adjustment such as hours worked and transfers within firms might be limited in order to avoid dismissals when a firm faced severe declines in the demand for goods continuously over several years. The main purpose of this paper is to examine quantitatively the effectiveness and limits of alternative measures for avoiding dismissals in Japanese industries.

In Japan, many manufacturing industries, particularly
material-type industries such as the textile, wood,
chemical and steel industries, have reduced the number of
employees continuously since the late 1970s. In these
industries, reductions in employment are not so much of a
temporary or cyclical nature, but are secular changes due
to structural changes. Furthermore, these industries
consist mostly of larger firms. Workers in this size of
firm tend to quite less and remain longer in one
particular firm, mainly due to their "firm-specific
skills" and the functioning of trade unionism.[2] These
tendencies are called the "internalization of labor" into
specific firms. The firms with more internal labor might
be limited to reducing the number of employees solely by
natural attrition, and might be under pressure to make
dismissals when faced by severe recessions.[3] It is also
possible that there might be some trade-off between
notices to quit and dismissals in internal labor markets.

According to recent research,[4] the two-thirds increase
in unemployment is attributed to structural changes and
institutional changes in the Japanese labor market, but
the displacement of labor directly caused by technological change does not seem to have any significant
impact on this change in unemployment. Rather, it whould
be noted that the increase in structural unemployment has
remained at maximum one percent, in spite of rapid
technological changes and a great number of sectoral
shifts in employment over the last decade. The flexible
internal adjustments within firms might have been effective in avoiding drastic displacements of employment and
in lowering technological unemployment. On the other
hand, the so called "life-time employment practice" in
Japan has become so well known, that it is apt to be
misunderstood, for instance the belief that Japanese
firms never dismiss workers, at least regularly contracted workers. But this is not true. Many firms, even
larger firms, can not avoid dismissing workers in severe
recessions. To examine quantitatively the effectiveness

and limits of alternative measures to dismissals would contribute not only to understanding the possible effects of technological change on employment and unemployment, but also to remedying the misunderstandings about Japanese labor practices.

In the following sections we will first examine the relationships between productivity changes and employment changes among manufacturing industries. Second, in section III, we will observe to what extent dismissals have occurred over time in the process of the reduction in employment in the manufacturing sector as a whole and in certain individual industries. Third, we will investigate quantitatively the substitutability of various alternatives to dismissals by estimating regression equations across the cross-section data divided by 20 two-digit manufacturing industries and the production levels. The paper's final section offers some concluding remarks.

II Productivity and Employment

One of the main effects of technological change is to promote labor productivity. The higher productivity leads not only to a direct savings in the number of man-hours required to produce a given output, but would also increase the demand for a good by lowering its cost and price. The net effect of the change in productivity on employment depends mainly on the elasticity of demand for each product with regard to its price. Because we cannot control for the other relevant variables such as the level and growth rate of aggregate real income, the conditions in international trade and so on, we cannot predict a priori any certain relationships between changes in productivity and changes in employment. However, to observe these relationships among industries in the long run would give us some persepectives on the structure of industry at a certain stage of economic development in Japan.

Figure 1 shows the various relationships between average annual rates of change in productivity measured in terms of value added per person, employed persons, GDP deflator and real GDP across 8 manufacturing industries during the 1954-73 period. Figure 2 shows these relationship across 11 industries during the 1973-81 period. From these figures, first, we could not find any clear relationships between changes in productivity and changes in employment either in the period before 1973 or after 1973, although the higher the change in productivity, the lower the price of goods, and the higher the growth of output measured by real GDP among manufacturing industries.

Second, we find the significant change that many manufacturing industries such as textile, pulp, primary metal and chemical industries have reduced total employment after 1973, while most industries increased employment rapidly before 1973.

Third, while the overall rates of change in productivity and employment have decreased in the entire manufacturing sector after 1973, as compared with before 1973, machine-type industries such as electrical machinery and transportation equipment industries have gained a higher or similar rate of growth in productivity after 1973 than before 1973. This higher growth in productivity in the machine-type industries including the precision machinery industry seems to reflect the "micro-electronics revolution". Its effect on employment is likely to be positive, but it will not be large enough to be able to increase the overall employment level in the manufacturing sector as a whole.

Figure 1. Productivity, Employment, Output and Prices
in Japanese Manufacturing Industries before
1973
(average annual rate of change during 1954-
1973)

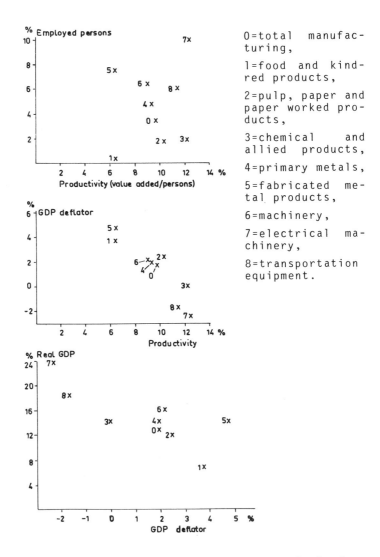

0=total manufac-
turing,

1=food and kind-
red products,

2=pulp, paper and
paper worked pro-
ducts,

3=chemical and
allied products,

4=primary metals,

5=fabricated me-
tal products,

6=machinery,

7=electrical ma-
chinery,

8=transportation
equipment.

source: Economic Planning Agency, Economic Analysis
(Keizai Bunseki), 57(1975,September)

Design: Muramatsu
Graphicdesign: IFEP Freiburg i.Br. Kö 87.2

Figure 2. Productivity, Employment, Output, and Price in Janpanese Manufacturing Industries after 1973

(average annual rate of change during 1973-1981)

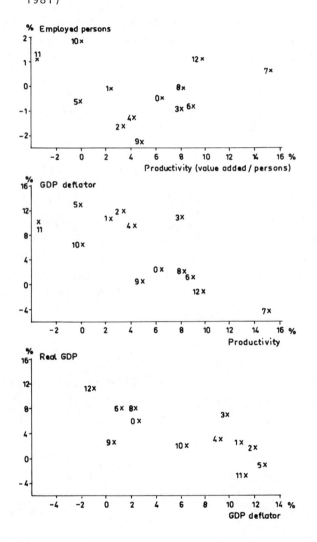

note: 0 to 8 are same as in Figure 1. 9=textile mill products, 10=petroleum and coal products, 11=ceramic, stone and clay products, 12=precision machinery.

source: Economic Planning Agency, Annual Report on National Accounts

Design: Muramatsu
Graphicdesign: IFEP Freiburg i. Br. Kö 87.2

III Employment and Dismissals

What kind of adjustments in the process of reducing
employment have been made since 1973? Figure 3 shows the
level and fluctuations in employment, hours worked,
output and productivity measured by output per manhour in
the manufacturing sector as a whole for establishments of
30 and more employees during 1970-82 period. From this
figure, we can make the following findings: First, the
recession just after the first oil crisis was the most
severe, and the effect on employment of the second oil
crisis in 1979-80 was less significant.

Second, during the recession following the first oil
crisis, the change in hours worked and the intensity of
work measured by the change in productivity have absorbed
much of the shock of the decrease in output, so that the
decline in employment was moderate and slow. The
relatively slower adjustment in employment seems to have
contributed to the less rapid increase in the rate of
unemployment in Japan than that in the U.S. and other
countries.

To what extend have dismissals taken place in the process
of reducing employment? Could dismissals be avoided by
using other measures such as restrictions on recruitments
and transfers within a firm? Figure 4 shows the trend and
fluctuations in various labor turnover rates for regularly contracted workers in the manufacturing sector for
establishments of 5 employees and more during the 1972-81
period. Regularly contracted workers are defined as the
employees who are employed with a definite contract of
not less than one year. Temporary and daily-employed
workers are excluded from them.

From this figure, we can make the following findings:
first, for regularly contracted male workers, the peak
rate of dismissal was 2 percent, and for female workers
it was 3 percent in 1975. Compared with the permanent

layoff rates (layoffs minus recalls) in the U.S., these rates are still lower, but it is noted that dismissals could not be avoided completely, as firms resorted to employment reductions when severe recessions occurred.

Second, transfers to other establishments within a firm not under pressure to dismiss employees have tended to increase just after recessions particularly for male employees, though the extent is not so significant.

How about in the individual industries? Even in the electrical equipment industry, which has increased employment in the long run (Figure 5-a), dismissals occurred to a considerable extent in 1974-75, particularly for female workers. This fact shows that the dismissals were not always limited to a few declining industries.

In the textile industry, which has continued to reduce employment (Figure 5-b), the dismissal rates are very much related to the decreasing rates of employment measured by the net separation rate. But the peak rate of dismissals was still 3 percent both for male and female workers. The restrictions on new recruitment seem to have contributed more to reduced employment than the dismissals.

In comparisons among selected industries which have reduced employment (Figure 5-c), the highest dismissal rate for male workers reached around 3 percent, which was not as high as expected. Although quit rates are lower in the chemical and steel industries, the dismissal rates seem to be no higher in these industries than in the lumber & wood and ceramic industries. The higher rates of transfer within a firm, particularly in the chemical industry, might contribute to lower dismissal rates.

Figure 3. Employment, Hours Worked and Output in Total
Manufacturing Sector during 1973-82
(index: 1973=100)

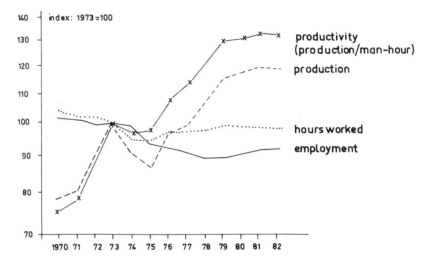

note: Employment and hours worked indices are based
only on regularly employed workers in the establishments with 30 and more employees.

source: Ministry of Labor, Monthly Labor Survey (Maigetsu
Kinro Tokei Chosa) and Ministry of Int. Trade &
Industry, Index of Industry and Mining (Kokogyo
Shisu Soran).

Figure 4.   Labor Turnover Rates in Total Manufacturing
            Sector during 1972-81
            (Regularly contracted workers)

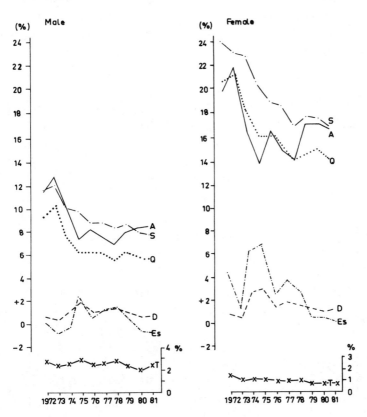

source: Ministry of Labor, Employment Trends Survey (Koyo
         Doko Chosa)

note: A = Accession rate, S = Separation rate, D = Dis-
         missal rate, Q = Quit rate, Ns = Net separation
         rate, T = transfer rate within firms (right
         scale). Labor turnover rates are annual and are
         based on the firms with establishments of 5 and
         more employees.

Design: Muramatsu	
Graphicdesign: IFEP Freiburg i.Br.	Kö 87.2

Figure 5-a. Labor Turnover Rates in Electrical Equipment
           Industry
           (regularly contracted workers)

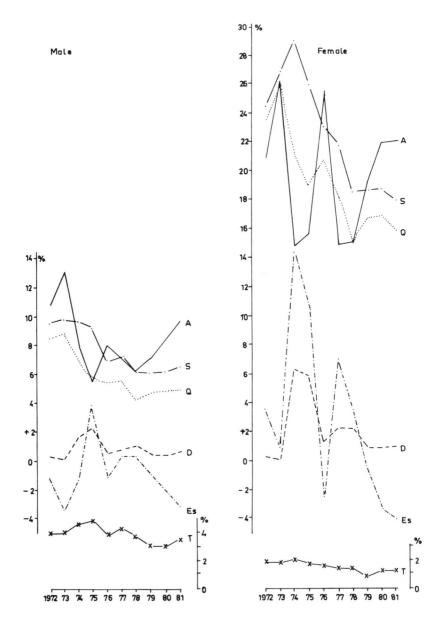

note and source: see Figure 4.

Design: Muramatsu
Graphicdesign: IFEP Freiburg i. Br. Kö 87.2

Figure 5-b. Labor Turnover Rates in Textile Industry
(regularly contracted workers)

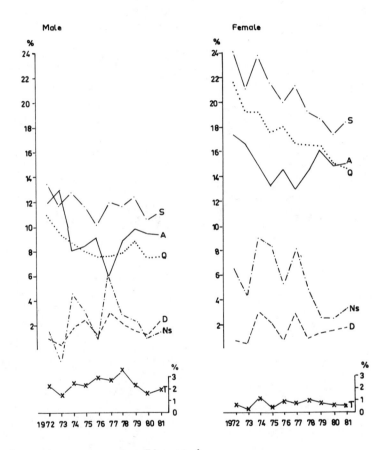

note and source: see Figure 4.

Design: Muramatsu
Graphicdesign: IFEP Freiburg i. Br. Kö 87.2

24

Figure 5-c. Labor Turnover Rates in Selected "Declining"
Industries
(regularly contracted workers)

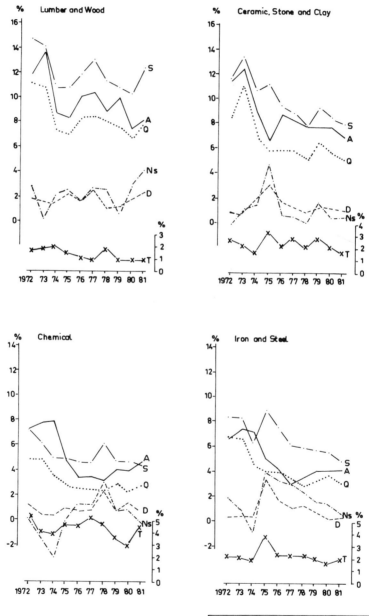

note and source: see Figure 4.

Design: Muramatsu
Graphicdesign: IFEP Freiburg i. Br. | Kö 87.2

From these observations, we could obtain some findings concerning the levels and fluctuations in dismissals, the relationships between dismissal rates and changes in employment, and other turnover rates. But we could make no determinations of the more rigorous relationships between dismissal rates and the changes in man-hours, or the extent of substitutability of various measures for dismissal.

IV Dismissal and its Alternatives

We will examine the following two points quantitatively by regression analysis using the cross-section data divided by 20 two-digit manufacturing industries and the production levels.

(1) The responsiveness of dismissal rate to the extent of the reduction in labor input (=man-hour)

(2) The substitutability of various alternatives for dismissals

    a) the proportional change in hours worked (H)

    b) the proportional change in temporary workers including part-time workers (Nt)

    c) accession rate (A)

    d) quit rate including separation rates but excluding dismissals (Q)

    e) the rate of net transfer to other related firms (To)

    f) the rate of net transfer to other establishments within a firm (Ti)

By definition, we get the following identities:

$$I = H + E$$

$$E = Wr (A - Q - D - Ti - To) + Wt\, Nt.$$

Hence,

$$D = -\frac{1}{Wr}\, I + \frac{1}{Wr}\, H + A - Q - Ti - To + \frac{Wt}{Wr}\, Nt, \qquad (1)$$

where

I : the proportional change of labor input (= man-hour)

E : the proportional change in the total number of employees

D : the rate of dismissal for regularly contracted workers

Wr : the fraction of regularly contracted workers to all workers

Wt : 1 - Wr.

There are, by definition, some substitutional relation- ships between dismissal rate and other variables when the proportional change in labor input is held. Hence, we could not estimate directly the relationships between dismissal rate and other variables. We then examined the substitutional relationships indirectly by estimating the effects on each variable of the proportional change of labor input and other structural factors which might be relevant to the relative costs of dismissals and others.

Hypothesis: A larger sized firm and a lower proportion of female workers strengthens the commitment of workers to specific firms mainly due to the aspect of firm- specific skills ("internalization of labor") and the demand for employment security by trade unions. Hence, the esta- blishments characterized by these factors would restrict the "external mobility" such as accessions, quits and dismissals, and utilize more the methods of "internal adjustment", such as altering the hours worked and transferring workers, and hiring temporary workers, in order to secure the employment of regular workers.

Data Source

We use The Employment Fluctuations Survey (Koyo Hendo Sogo Chosa) conducted by the Ministry of Labor of Japan in 1978, which gives the data for the proportional changes in the various components of labor input from

March in 1975 to March in 1978 at the aggregated
establishments divided into 20 two-digit industries and
the production changes during the period (4 partitions).

Specification in Estimation

Dependent variables:
    each component in the equation (1), which is measured
    as the proportional changes from March in 1975 to
    March in 1978.

Independent variables:
(1) the proportional change in labor input (I) : the
    proxy of demand for labor.
(2) the square of I : approximation of non-linear
    relations with non-negative restrictions in some
    variables.
(3) log. of average scale of establishment (S) : the
    proxy of scale of firm : the factor which would
    promote "internalization of labor" from the aspect of
    management and labor relations.
(4) the fraction of female workers in regularly contrac-
    ted workers (F) : which would decrease the extent of
    "internalization of labor" from the aspect of diffe-
    rent behavior of the labor supply.
(5),(6) the interaction terms of each S times I and F
    times I : the responsiveness of each variable to the
    changes in labor input could be different with
    respect to the levels of S land F.

The Results of the Estimation (Table 1 and Fig. 6-8)

The overall extent of the explanation was not as good as
expected. Though there remain some questionable points
about data and estimation, we could get the following
findings:

TABLE 1. Regressions for Various Components of Labor Input : Cross Section Data for Manufacturing Industries by 2-Digit and Production Level

Dependent Variables / Coefficient of:	Dismissal rate (D)	Accession rate (A)	Quit rate (Q)	Net Transfer Within(Ti)	Net Transfer Outside(To)	Net Transfer $\frac{1}{Wr}\cdot H$ a)	$\frac{Wt}{Wr}$ Nt b)	Weighted Mean S.D.
Proportional Change of Labor Input (I)	-0.830 (3.62)**	1.03 (1.52)	0.655 (1.29)	-0.0034 (0.03)	0.131 (1.38)	-0.214 (1.17)	0.165 (1.21)	0.0030 / 0.113
(I)²	0.548 (2.48)**	1.69 (2.59)**	1.59 (3.25)**	-0.0133 (0.11)	0.0050 (0.06)	0.145 (0.82)	0.216 (1.64)	0.0126 / 0.016
Fraction of Female Workers (F)	0.0171 (0.80)	0.539 (8.49)**	0.451 (9.51)**	0.0288 (2.53)**	-0.0077 (0.87)	-0.067 (3.88)**	0.031 (2.41)**	0.338 / 0.173
(F)*(I)	0.295 (1.64)	0.972 (1.82)*	-0.351 (0.88)	0.0953 (1.00)	0.0385 (0.52)	-0.216 (1.49)	-0.011 (1.02)	0.0013 / 0.045
Log. of Average Scale Of Establishment(S)	-0.0112 (1.62)	-0.0317 (1.54)	-0.0079 (0.51)	0.0089 (2.40)**	0.0088 (3.07)**	0.0141 (2.54)**	-0.0008 (0.18)	3.40 / 0.54
(S)*(I)	0.167 (2.84)**	-0.166 (0.95)	-0.106 (0.82)	-0.0241 (0.77)	-0.0472 (1.94)*	0.136 (2.90)**	-0.0044 (0.13)	0.016 / 0.39
Constant Term	0.102	0.297	0.201	-0.0358	-0.0198	0.0134	-0.0005	
R²	0.314	0.712	0.621	0.140	0.126	0.558	0.364	
S.E.	0.0309	0.0914	0.0682	0.0164	0.0128	0.0247	0.0184	
Weighted Mean S.D.	0.0765 / 0.037	0.394 / 0.170	0.346 / 0.111	0.0036 / 0.018	0.0073 / 0.014	0.042 / 0.037	0.0103 / 0.023	

note: ( ) :t value, *: significant at the 0.10 level, **: significant at the 0.05 level,

Proportional change and turnover rates are measured from March in 1975 to March in 1978. Weighted least squares method with the number of establishment as weight. The number of observations: 80.

a) $\frac{1}{Wr}H$: the proportional change of hours worked divided by the fraction of regular workers

b) $\frac{Wt}{Wr}Nt$: the ratio of temporary/regular workers times the proportional change of temporary workers (including part-time workers)

Data source: Ministry of Labor, Employment Fluctuations Survey (Koyo hendo Sogo Chosa) 1979)

Figure 6. Estimated Change Rates in Components of Labor
Input for the Proportional Change in Labor
Input

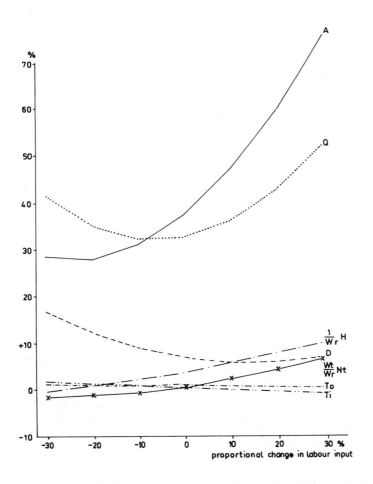

note: The estimates are based on the regression equations in Table 1 given S = 3.40 and F = 0.338
which are weighted mean.

Design: Muramatsu

Graphicdesign: IFEP Freiburg i. Br. | Kö 87.2

Figure 7. Estimated Effects of an Increase of Establishment Size on Each Component of Labor Input

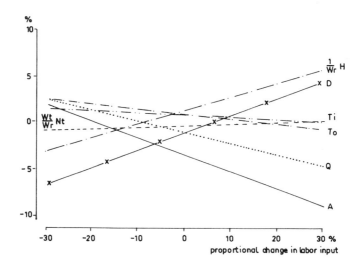

note: Based on the regression equations in Table 1,
the estimates of each component are the changes
from the average (Figure 6) when establishment
size increases from 30 employees (S = 1.08) to
88 employees (S = 4.48).

Design: Muramatsu

Graphicdesign: IFEP Freiburg i.Br. Kö 87.2

Figure 8. Estimated Effects of an Increase of Female-
Fraction on Each Component of Labor Input

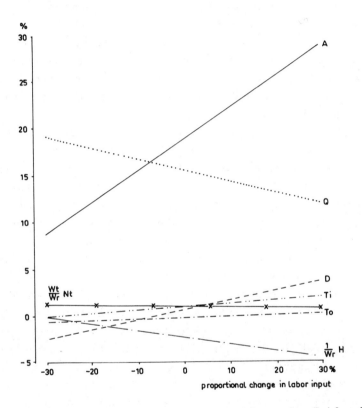

note: Based on the regression equations in Table 1,
the estimates of each component are the changes
from the average (Figure 6) when the fraction
of female workers (F) increases from 0.338 to
0.684.

| Design: Muramatsu |
| Graphicdesign: IFEP Freiburg i.Br. Kö 87.2 |

(1) When the size of an establishment and the fraction of female workers are fixed at the average level, the contribution of the accession rate to the change in labor input is likely to be more relevant, and that of the dismissal rate becomes larger as the labor input decreases by more than 10 percent.

(2) As for the substitutability of various measures for dismissal, those of transfers within and outside firms were very small, and that of hours worked was a little larger, but not statistically significant. These measures of internal adjustment seem to be not as significant as expected over a longer period of three years, though these might be more effective in the shorter term, such as periods less than one year.

(3) The substitutability of temporary workers for regularly contracted workers was not as significant as usually expected when the change rate of temporary workers is adjusted by the ratio of temporary to regular workers. While temporary workers tend to fluctuate more frequently than regularly contracted workers, this fact does not contribute very much to the changes in manhours, since the ratio of temporary workers to all workers is not very large.

(4) Rather, the quit rate is likely to become the most substitutable for the dismissal rate among the various measures, as the quit rate tends to turn upward significantly when the reduction in manhours becomes greater than 10 percent. This finding, which was not expected beforehand, might reflect that the workers at firms with poor perspectives tend to leave voluntarily. Or, considering that the separation due to retirement is included in this quit rate, this might mean that firms in difficulties urge older workers to retire before the normal age in order to avoid dismissals.

(5) As the size of the establishment becomes larger, the contribution of hours worked and the contribution of transfers and temporary workers to the change in labor input increase, and the dismissal rate decreases. Therefore the substitutional relationships of these

measures for dismissals could be determined to some extent.

(6) As the fraction of female workers becomes larger, the external mobility such as quits and accessions increases and the contibution of hours worked decreases. But the effect of these contributions on the dismissal rate is not certain.

V Concluding Remarks

Since 1973, Japanese manufacturing industries, mainly the material type industries such as textile, chemical, and iron & steel, have reduced employment secularly rather than cyclically, not due to the rapid changes in productivity, but due to the secular changes in the stage of industrialization or the comparative advantage in international trade. In the process of reducing employment, dismissals were substantial and increased particularly during the recession of 1974-75. The levels of the dismissal rate, however, were still lower. One of the reasons for the lower dismissals, as mentioned, could be that firms have utilized the internal adjustments such as hours worked, intensity of work and transfers within firms or to other related firms as far as possible in order to avoid dismissals.

But according to our estimation, the extent of substitutability of these internal adjustments for dismissals was quantitatively not as great as usually expected in the representative manufacturing establishment, in which the size of the establishments is generally smaller. Although the larger the size of the establishment, the greater the substitution tended to be, even the larger establishments could not avoid dismissals when the necessary reduction in labor input rose to more than 20 percent for three years after 1975.

Fortunately, the recession after the second oil crisis, 1979-80, was not very severe in Japan, so that "declining industries" could reduce employment mainly by attritions and internal adjustments. This contributed to an increase in the rate of unemployment in Japan that was less rapid than in other western countries. But we should not overestimate the substitutability on internal adjustments for dismissals.

Finally, we have to say that this paper focused mainly on the quantity of dismissals, but did not examine in detail the crucial problem of "who is dismissed?". The social impact of dismissal would be different depending not only on the quantity of dismissals but also on the quality of dismissals such as the criteria for selecting who will be let go. In Japan, the criteria for dismissals seem to be unclear, not like the seniority system in the U.S.. Instead, the middle-aged and older workers tend to be dismissed relatively more often than junior workers.[5] This tendency has brought about serious social problems, such as relatively higher unemployment rates for older workers. These problems remain as tasks for the future.

Footnotes

1) See the following literature: Hideko Shinozuka, Emiko
Ishihara, "Oil shock Iko no Koyochosei (Employment
Adjustment since Oil Shock)", Nihon Keizai Kenkyu No. 6
(Sept. 1977). Haruo Shimada et al., "Chingin Oyobi
Koyochosei Katei no Bunseki (The Analysis of Wage and
Employment Adjustment Process)", Keizai Bunseki 84
(August 1982). K.Muramatsu, Nihon no Rodoshijou Bunseki
(The Analysis of Labor Market in Japan) Hakutoshobo,
1983.

2) See Richard B.Freeman, "The Exit-Voice in the Labor
Market: Unionism, Job Tenure, Quits, and Separations",
Quarterly Journal of Economics 88 (June 1980) and K.Mura-
matsu, "Rishoku Kodo to Rodokumiai (Quit Behavior and
Trade Unions) in Kazuo Koike ed. Gendai no Shitsugyou
(Contemporary Unemployment) Dobunkan, forthcoming.

3) According to James L.Medoff, "Layoffs and Alternatives
under Trade Unions in U.S. Manufacturing", American
Economic Review 69 (June 1979), the lower quit rates in
the unionized sector is considered to be one of the
reasons for higher layoff rates in that sector in the
U.S..

4) See Ministry of Labor, Rodo Hakusho (White Paper on
Labor 1983).

5) See Kazuo Koike, "Kaiko kara mita Gendai Nippon no
Roshikankei (Contemporary Industrial Relations from the
aspect of Dismissal)", in Kyoto Institute of Economic
Research ed. Nihon Keizai no Kozo Bunseki (The Structural
Analysis of Japanese Economy) Sobunsha, forthcoming.

A Comment on
Professor K. Muramatsu's
Productivity, Employment and Turnover
in Japanese Manufacturing Industries"

Friedrich L. Sell

The author's aim is to explain how the rate of unemployment in Japan's manufacturing industries[1] has increased less rapidly than in the U.S. or other OECD-countries during the two severe recession periods in the seventies. This he attributes to:

- restrictions on recruitments
- transfer of workers to other establishments of the firm
- transfer to other related firms
- a change in the number of hours worked
- a change in the number of temporary workers
- etc.

According to Muramatsu, it is the main purpose of his paper to examine quantitatively the effectiveness and limits of alternative measures for avoiding dismissals in Japanese industries. Therefore, this review of Prof. Muramatsu's paper will concentrate on chapter IV: "Dismissal and its Alternatives".

In section IV, the author develops his equation (1) which contains only definitions and/or identities:

$$(1) \quad D = \frac{-1}{W_R} I + \frac{1}{W_R} H + A - Q - T_i - T_o + \frac{Wt}{W_R} Nt$$

with

D = the rate of dismissal for regularly contracted workers

W_R = the ratio of regularly contracted workers
to all workers

Wt = $1 - W_R$

I = growth rate of hours worked (W_{std}) in one year

H = growth rate of hours worked per employee
$W (\frac{std}{E})$

E = growth rate in the number of employees (W_E)

A = accession rate

Q = quit rate

To = the rate of net transfer to other related firms

Ti = the rate of net transfer to other establishments
within a firm

Nt = the proportional change in the number of temporary workers, including part-time workers

It will be shown in the following that Prof. Muramatsu's
equation (1) can be rewritten in a modified version
- which will include two new aspects for the dismissal
rate - if one considers another tautological relationship
(see E. Knappe, 1979, p. 25):

$$(2) \quad W_{Std} = W_{ym} - W (\frac{ym}{std})$$

with

W_{Std} = I = growth rate of hours worked in one year
(see above)

W_{ym} = growth rate of the net social product at market prices

$W \left(\frac{ym}{std} \right)$ = growth rate of the working hour productivity

Equating (2) with Prof. Muramatsu's equation,

$$(3) \quad \underbrace{W_{std}}_{I} \quad = \quad \underbrace{W_E}_{E} \quad + \quad \underbrace{W \left(\frac{Std}{E} \right)}_{H}$$

one arrives at (after rearranging)

$$(1^*) \quad D^* \quad = \quad (A - Q - Ti - To) + \frac{Wt}{W_R} \ Nt + \frac{1}{W_R} \ W \left(\frac{Std}{E} \right)$$

$$- \frac{1}{W_R} \ W_{ym} \ + \frac{1}{W_R} \ W \left(\frac{ym}{std} \right)$$

Although Prof. Muramatsu is quite right when he claims that there are some substitutional relationships between dismissal rate and other variables when the proportional change of labour input (is) fixed, it might be useful not to "exclude" a priori the

- working hour productivity and
- the growth rate of the NSP, each weighted by the ratio of regular workers.

Why?

(i) First, because Prof. Muramatsu's approach is fully supply-oriented, whereas the recessions after the two oil-crises had a cost-push and a demand-collapse-effect!

(ii) Second, the relationship between the working hour productivity and the size of the firm or the proportion of female workers should be investigated.

When specifying his estimation equations, Prof. Muramatsu takes the growth rate of labour input as a proxy for demand for labour; would it not make more sense to derive demand for labour from total demand?

Following Prof. Muramatsu, the larger firms have a ratio of temporary workers to all workers which lies significantly above the average. If their labour productivity - measured by the productivity of hours worked - is significantly higher than the productivity of the regular workers [2], it must be taken into account that:

(4) $\dfrac{y}{std} = \dfrac{y}{E} \cdot \dfrac{E}{std}$

(5) $E = R + T$

R = Regular workers
T = Temporary workers

so that

(4a) $\dfrac{y}{std} = \dfrac{y}{(R + T)} \cdot \left(\dfrac{R}{std} + \dfrac{T}{std} \right)$ or

(4b) $\dfrac{y}{std} = \dfrac{1}{\dfrac{R}{y} + \dfrac{T}{y}} \cdot \left(\dfrac{1}{\dfrac{std}{R}} + \dfrac{1}{\dfrac{std}{T}} \right)$

This would imply that - other things being equal - larger firms show a labour productivity which is significantly above the mean value during the prosperous part of the business cycle.
Thus, when dismissing temporary workers in the recession, larger firms are in a better position to hoard regular workers.

Add to this Prof. Muramatsu's assumption that those firms which have a lower proportion of female (regular) workers employ more (regular) male workers with firm-specific skills than others do. Again, it can be argued that if

$$(6) \quad R = R_M + R_F \, ,$$

labour productivity is given by

$$(4c) \quad \frac{y}{std} = (\frac{y}{R_M + R_F}) \cdot (\frac{R_M}{std} + \frac{R_F}{std}) \quad \text{or}$$

$$(4d) \quad \frac{y}{std} = (\frac{y}{R_M + R_F}) \cdot (\frac{1}{\frac{std}{R_M}} + \frac{1}{\frac{std}{R_F}})$$

If labour productivity of female (regular) workers is above the mean value $1/(\frac{R}{y})$, a lower proportion of female workers during a recession increases - other things being equal - the possibilities of internal transfer of work or of reduction of hours worked per employee in order to avoid the dismissal of regular male workers.

In respect to the final demand argument (see above), it is worthwhile to note that Prof. Muramatsu expects a lowering of production costs and thus of the price - when technological changes have taken place - and a subsequent increase in demand depending on the price elasticity. What he did not investigate, however, is the question to what extent a lower growth rate of the GNP affects the demand for manufactured goods, i.e. the income elasticities of demand!

Furthermore, a lowering of the production prices can only be expected when there is strong competition between the producers; otherwise, they could try as

well to increase their profit rate in response to lower
production costs.[3]

On the other hand, within declining industries - as
Japans textile industry - it can often be observed that
there is a "marching in step" instead of strict
competition!

As far as Prof. Muramatsu's estimation results are
concerned, I only would like to state the following
points:

(i) The proportion of female (regular) workers has a
      significant impact on almost all the dependent
      variables considered by Prof. Muramatsu, but I
      could not find much of an explanation for this fact
      in his paper.

(ii) All the estimated relationships have in common the
      fact that the achieved R^2 is rather poor. Thus, it
      can be presumed that important explanatory factors
      are missing. This can justify to some extent the
      omission of the Durbin-Watson-statistic.

(iii) The graphs of figure (6) - for example the parabola
      of the accession rate - can be interpreted as
      partial relationships of the form:

      (7) $\hat{A}$ = constant term + 1,03 I + 1,69 I^2

      in which the remaining explanatory variables (F,S,
      etc.) are assumed constant.

(iv) Neither in figure (7) nor in figure (8) is the
      transition from small to big establishment sizes,
      or from a small proportion of (regular) female
      workers to a high proportion clear. Should there
      not be two graphs for each (dependent) variable:

one for the "floor-value" of size proportion and another for the "ceiling value"?

Summing up, the most interesting aspect of Prof. Muramatsu's paper was the explanation of "internal adjustments" in Japanese firms as an alternative to dismissals, and as an important factor in Japan's lower rate of unemployment in comparison with other OECD-countries.

It is of particular interest that the author has done a comprehensive study which focuses on a multidimensional quantitative analysis of a highly complex phenomenon. As such studies are quite rare, the author deserves recognition for his valuable contribution.

References

KNAPPE, E.: Arbeitszeitverkürzung - Ein geeignetes Mittel zur Überwindung der Arbeitslosigkeit?, in: WISU 1/79, S. 25-31.

ROPPEL, U.: Vollbeschäftigung auch bei reduziertem Wachstum?, in: Der Bürger im Staat, Heft 4/1980, S. 242-248.

Footnotes

1) material (textile, chemicals and iron + steel) industries.

2) This assumption has not been made by Prof. Muramatsu although it is probably necessary for his later conclusions.

3) The GDP-Deflator might not be an adequate measure for the prices of goods from manufacturing industries.

Unemployment and Reduction of Working Hours
- Measurement, Impacts, Costs -

Siegfried Hauser

1 Arithmetical Approach

The following reasons are given to explain the correlation between the level of employment and the reduction in working hours: in 1970, there were 22.2 million employees in the Federal Republic of Germany; they worked 41.5 hours per week which adds up to 921.3 million hours of working volume; there were almost no unemployed persons [1]. In 1982, we had 22.4 million employees who worked 40.1 hours a week with a total working volume of 898.2 hours. In equating this working volume with the existing demand for labor in the economy, and in including in the labor supply 1.8 million unemployed persons for 1982, we find that at a level of 37.1 working hours, supply and demand correspond arithmetically to each other - so there should be no unemployment. Moreover, if we take into account an annual productivity growth per employee of + 2 % for 1982, the above-mentioned balance is reached at 36.4 hours. Continuing this calculation up to September 1983, we can state that the number of unemployed persons rose to 2.1 million, and within the first nine months of the same year, the average productivity growth observed was 2.4 % [2]. Thus the arithmetical balance is reached at 35.8 hours. In this view, the weekly working volume consists of a product of the number of employees B and the working hours per week h. As the number of employees is given, only working time varies. [3].

These simple arithmetical examples require discussion, during which we assume that either a constant labor supply is combined with a shrinking demand for labor, or there is an increasing labor supply and a constant labor demand.

2 Possibilities offered and problems caused by a reduction of working hours

2.1 Possibilities offered by a reduction of working hours

The following possibilities to reduce working hours seem to me to be realistic: We can subdivide them into general measures - that is measures concerning all employees -, selective measures concerning only certain groups of employees with determined characteristics, and individual measures, which is the case when decisions are to be taken by the individual himself:

(1) General measures

- Measures concerning work life as a whole [4]
  = delaying the beginning of work life by the introduction of a tenth compulsory school year or one year of basic professional preparation;
  = interrupting ones work life by undertaking retraining courses and supplementary education, long vacation proportional to the length of service (Sabbatical), extending special maternity regulations, introducing a baby year;
  = earlier retirement by means of a general lowering of the pension retirement age, granting an earlier retirement pay, lowering the flexible age limit;

- Measures concerning periodical working time
  = reduction of weekly working hours
  = restriction or prohibition of overtime hours
  = increase in part-time work
  = job-sharing
  = prolongation of annual vacation or the introduction of an annual training vacation [5].

(2) Selective Measures

While the reasons given in favor of general measures are mostly of a political nature, the arguments for selective measures are based on reasons of health policy (shift-work, night-work, maternity regulations), social politics (retirement, baby-year, education, supplementary education, retraining courses) or are of an ethical nature (free time as a value in itself, a right to work).

(3) Individual Measures

The individual's possibilities to reduce his working hours can apply on the flexibilization of working hours per week, per year or to the total number of hours to be spent working by an individual in his life [6]. In this way the "Santa-Clara-treaty" in the U.S.A. enables company members to apply for a reduction in their working hours by 5 %, 10 % or 20 % with a corresponding reduction in wages. Job-sharing models are in a few cases also practiced in Germany. In France, the model of a "one year working contract" with flexible arrangements within this quota is being discussed, and in part already realized. In addition to this, models of "flexible retirement" are being considered in France, Sweden, Switzerland and Germany.

2.2 Problems in the practical arrangement of a reduction in working hours

When measures to reduce working hours are carried out, frictions necessarily appear in regard to regional and sectoral structures as well as frictions implied by differing expert qualification and differing sizes of companies. Thus, regional divergences in the unemployment rate are considerable [7]. In Lower Saxony, the ratio of unemployed persons to available jobs is 36 : 1, whereas in Baden-Württemberg this ratio is only 12 : 1.

Imbalances similar to the above mentioned also appear in the <u>sectoral</u> allotment of unemployment [8]. There is for example, one free job for 6.7 unemployed persons in the banking and insurance branch, one job for 24.2 unemployed in the manufacturing industry, and in the power industry. In the water supply and in mining there are even 50.6 unemployed persons applying for each free job. A first reference to the difficulties implied by the qualification structure of unemployment shows up in column "other unemployed" [9]; here there are 589.9 unemployed for one free job.

The differences in the qualification structure show up even more clearly if we examine the unemployed in respect to their professional qualification. Considering the gainfully employed with professional qualification, there is one free job for 12.7 unemployed persons but for unskilled workers there are 43.4 unemployed applying for one job, which is more than three times as many [10]. The problem of imbalance appears not only in the existing professional qualification structure, but it arises already for persons beginning their profession; for example there are considerable divergences if we take university graduates into account. The imbalance for artists is 6.9 %, for teachers 17.6 %, for economic and social scientists and for electrical engineers it is 32 %, and for mathematicians it sums up to 46.1 % [11].

Moreover, in redistributing work, one has to consider that there are specific sex and age divergencies in unemployment [12] as well as problems caused by the size of enterprice [13]. In my opinion, all the problems broached can be resolved because they are - so to speak with inversed signs - similar to the problems involved in increasing employment with the only difference that now there is not an additional, but a shrinking demand for labor. It is hard to determine an optimum structure of working hours for employees, from which less optimal arrangements concerning a general reduction of working hours could be derived. In this context, it is "perhaps not redundant to emphasize that economical problems always appear as a result of variations. As long as there is no variation or at least as long as everything develops in the expected way, there will not appear new problems which demand a decision and there will be no necessity to set up a new plan. The argument that variations, or at least daily adaptations, are nowadays less important includes the statement that also economical problems have become less important" [14].

2.3 Problem of wage adjustment

In regard to wage adjustment in the frame of reduction of working hours, we have to consider the wage rate (1), the price level (p) and the productivity ( ). We distinguish among the following cases:

- a reduction of working hours (h) without a wage adjustment, where price and productivity increases are to be included in our analysis, that is, asking if $|\Delta h| \lesseqgtr \Delta p + \Delta \pi$ applies.

- a reduction of working hours with wage adjustment. Here, impacts of costs, redistribution and demand depend on the level of wage adjustment and on price and productivity increases.

We shall discuss the problems mentioned in the following section.

3   Impact of a reduction of working hours

3.1   Reduction of annual working hours

3.1.1   Impact on working performance and on unit costs

When working hours are to be reduced, enterprises can

only reduce the work volume per employee in the short
term. In spite of this we cannot assume a proportional
decline in working performance to the reduction of
working hours. Investigations of above mentioned
problem [15] lead to the conclusion that working performance decreases to a smaller extent than working hours,
due to reduced frequency of accidents, lower rate of
absence, reduction of underproportionate performance
times and a generally better performance disposition.

Such empirical investigations deduced from former experience with reduction of working hours, showed that the
majority of workers is anxious to keep the achieved level
of performance by increasing work input. In reducing
working hours from 8 to 6 hours a day, the daily
performance in exhausting physical work does not decrease
to a level of 75 %, but only to 90 % of previous performance.

Let us analyse the impact on unit costs, and more precisely on personnel expenditure which result from a
reduction of working hours. In the member countries of
the EEC, every three years since 1966 inquiries have been
carried out on working costs, the last of which was done
in 1981 [16]. In Germany in 1981, personnel expenditure
per employee [17], that is the remuneration for working
performance as well as additional personnel expenditure,
amounted to 46,729 DM. Compared with the figures from
1972, this means a total increase of 103.8 %, or an
average annual increase of 8.2 %. It must be remarked
that within the industry sector, divergencies are
considerable: Enterprises with 10 - 49 employees estimate
their personnel expenditure at 38,141 DM, showing an
increase of 91.5 % in comparison to the 1972 figures, and
an enterprise with 1000 and more employees estimates its
personnel expenditure at 53,573 DM with an increase of
114.5 % for the same period. In the shoe manufacturing
industry personnel expenditure rose to 29,762 DM,
including an increase of 86.1 %, and in the mineral oil

industry expenditure is 80,844 DM including an increase of 141.0 % in comparison to 1972. The highest increase in personnel expenditure was 165.4 % for the period mentioned, and occurred in the office machine and computer manufacturing branch. In total, the differences between branches increased; this development is expressed by a coefficient of variation of 18 % for 1972 and 25 % for 1981.

As a first result we can state that personnel expenditure differs greatly between the different branches and it develops according to the growth rate of the branch and the size of the enterprise. Thus, wage costs per manufactured unit show different impacts depending on the model used to reduce working hours; there seems to be some kind of inherent structural balance.

First of all, in the context of discussions on the reduction of working hours, we take only the remuneration for working performance into account, which in 1981 sums up to 26,630 DM or 57 % of total personnel expenditure spent by producing industry. Consequently, we can ascertain a cost increasing impact when measures to reduce working hours with wage adjustment are taken, if the increase in the wage rate per hour is higher than the growth in productivity and inflation rate, that is $\Delta l + \Delta p + \Delta \pi$. We have to pay attention to the fact that remuneration for working performance has risen in the producing industry between 1972 and 1981 by a mere 80.7 % - personnel expenditure increased in the same period by 103.8 % - and that this increase differed greatly, whereby, on the one hand, in enterprises with 10 - 49 employees the increase was 65.9 % and, on the other hand, in enterprises with 1000 and more employees it was 90.4 %. This means that the part of personnel expenditure mentioned increased in this period in an underproportionate manner.

This leads us to the other part of personnel expenditure,

the additional personnel expenditure. Additional personnel expenditure is a term summing up all costs incurred
beside normal remuneration for work offered. Such costs
include employer's contributions to compulsory social
insurance, compensation for free days, expenditure for
the company's pension scheme and special allowance.

First of all, we have to point out that personnel expenditure which amounted in 1981 to 20,099 DM and thus to
43 % of the total wage costs in producing industry,
increased between 1972 and 1981 by 145.4 %, which means
that the increase in additional personnel expenditure was
1.8 times higher than the increase in remuneration for
working performance.

In subdividing additional personnel expenditure into
costs which depend on production on the one hand, and, on
the other hand, costs which do not depend on production,
we can treat the first group as if they were a
remuneration for working performance - thus their cost
impacts depend on the price level and the productivity
increase when the reduction in working hours with wage
adjustment takes place - whereas additional personnel
expenditures not depending on production always have cost
increasing impacts when working hours are reduced.
Considering the employers' compulsory contributions to
social insurance, compensations for free days - not
counting official holidays - as well as special allow-
ances (bonus, holiday pay) as costs dependent on
production because they are mostly connected with the
remuneration [19], we state that these costs amount to
75.4 % of additional personnel expenditure [20], and this
amounts to 32.4 % of total personnel expenditure.
Additional personnel expenditure not depending on production - compensations for official holidays, company's
pension scheme, expenditure for staff's equipment,
private wealth accumulation, and other special services -
sum up to 24.6 % of total additional personnel expenditure. These costs signify 10.6 % of total personnel

expenditure, which means that a reduction in working hours from 40 to 35 hours a week, which is a decline of 12.5 %, would cause cost increases of about 1.5 %.

In order to complete the analysis of cost impacts when measures are taken to reduce working hours, we also have to take into account capital costs. In this context, a general statement is very hard to make as cost impact depends on the degree of capacity utilization, rationalization rate, rate of depreciation [21] and on job layout costs [22]. Yet if we dared analyse in a general way and assumed that 10-20 % of capital costs do not depend on production [23], a cost charge of 1.4-2.8 % would be the maximum average of an upper limit when introducing a 35-hour work-week.

3.1.2 Reflections on national economic demand

If one does not believe in the automatism of Say's law, we should add here some reflections on the total national economic demand to the above analysis of the cost aspect. "Keynes discovered in his analysis a simple error in Say's law in stating that Say mixed up the doubtlessly correct argument that any income from means of production derives from sales of production, with the uncorrect statement that all costs caused by production are in consequence necessarily covered by sales profits. The second statement is deduced by error from the first one ... . Businessmen probably base their sales expectations on present demand. This is the reason why they tend to reckon with sales profits breaking even with total costs of production" [24]. If a reduction in working hours without any wage adjustment took place, the result would probably be a decline in purchasing power, in which case the firms'sales expectations might be disappointed.

Starting from the fact that in 1982 [25] there were 22.4 million employees and 1.8 million unemployed, the sum of net wages amounted to 507.2 billion DM, and the unemployment benefits were 18.0 billion DM, then the total existant purchasing power summed up to 525.2 billion DM. If a 35-hour work-week without wage adjustment is introduced (reduction of working hours and wages by 12.5 %), there will be - if every unemployed person finds a job - a decline in purchasing power in the order of 44 billion DM or 8.3 %. One year before, in 1981, when there were only 1.3 million unemployed, and taking also the corresponding reference quantities into account, the purchasing power would have fallen by 51 billon DM or 9.9 %.

Thus it follows in the first place, that in the case of a reduction of working hours without wage adjustment, the purchasing power will decline less the higher the unemployment rate is. That means that there would be no decline in purchasing power when the rates of unemployment benefits and the decline in purchasing power balance out. In 1982, when we had a loss of purchasing power amounting to 44 billion DM, this effect would have shown up at a level of unemployment of 6 million, that is 4 million more unemployed than there actually were. The loss of purchasing power then already occurred.

If we include consumption rates in our reflections and look at the following table.

Consumption rates of different household types						
Type of household	1965	1970	Y e a r: 1975	1980	1981	1982
Household with 2 per-persons, receiving retirement pay or social assistance	94,1	91,8	88,8	86,9	85,0	85,0
Household with 4 persons with average income	88,6	86,7	81,9	81,6	79,9	81,7
Household with 4 persons civil servants and other employees receiving higher incomes.	80,3	78,6	74,9	76,1	72,5	72,1

Source: Statistisches Bundesamt (Ed.): Wirtschaft und Statistik 5/1983, Stuttgart, Mainz, 1983, page 450

We notice in the above mentioned table that the decline in the consumption rate in the lower income brackets has stopped since 1981, and for employees' households with 4 persons it has increased to the level attained in the mid-seventies.

As an another conclusion, we can reckon that when a reduction of working hours without wage adjustment takes place, the loss of purchasing power will be less sensitive than indicated in our model calculation because the consumption rate will increase.

Both conclusions neglect the aspect that the entire nation will be poorer and, as a comparison of consumption rates as a possible indicator reveals, distribution will be more unequal.

3.1.3 Remarks on the matter of wage adjustment

If we draw our conclusions from the facts mentioned above, we have to differentiate more distinctly in the question of wage adjustment when reducing working hours. As we formerly saw, personnel expenditure depending on production rises by 1.5 % and capital costs by an average of 2.1 % when working hours are reduced. Personnel expenditure in 1981 amounted to 331.2 billion DM and costs for depreciation, interest for borrowed capital, rents and leases, and other costs - here considered altogether as capital costs - summed up to 247.0 billion DM [26]. According to our observations in section 3.1.1, the total increase in costs not dependent on production would amount to about 10 billion DM for the whole economy when working time is reduced to 35 hours per week and without wage adjustment. In 1981, this figure is combined with a decline in purchasing power by 51 billion DM when no wage adjustment is undertaken. Taking into account the council of experts forecast for 1984, which predicts for this period a productivity rate of 2-2.5 % and a price increase rate of 3 % [27], and assuming the argument that a moderately high inflation rate is beneficial to economic growth, then we should consider neither total nor partial wage adjustment as completely negative.

3.2 Reduction of individual work life

Measures taken in favour of a reduction of individual work life are politically as well as in economic policy less contested than a reduction in working hours per week. There are, for example, the following measures: lowering the general level of the age limits for retirement, flexible age limits, introducing long vacations (Sabbatical), tenth compulsory school year, retraining courses to be repeated periodically, and introduction of a socalled baby-year are all applicable in this case. The most being said in the case of reduction of weekly working hours is valid in this case too. The impact of an employment policy depends on the adjustment behaviour of the enterprises and, even more precisely, on cost, productivity and demand impacts. In this case, costs cause less problems than the creation of new jobs does, and they do not involve further investments or costs occurred by lower capacity utilization as shown before in the case of a reduction in weekly working hours. So a job which becomes vacant by the above mentioned means could simply be taken by a new person. The risk involved for enterprises which adjust to the reduced working hours through overtime regulations is in this case smaller than it is when the weekly working hours are reduced. As far as compulsory contributions to social insurance to be paid by employers are not concerned, the costs are simply shifted to the public sector and consequently to the taxpayers, which could lead to an increase in the tax rate or in other government dues. Whether there is a demand deficit for the whole economy depends on the organization of the measures mentioned and on the consumption rates of the groups of persons concerned, and also possibly on the appearance of ratchet-effects. If measures to reduce work life by supplementary education are taken, we might expect a positive influence on productivity and technical progress.

4 Final Remarks

Discussions on the reduction of working hours should not be subject to emotional outbursts, but some of the comments usually made a strong resemblance to them. In Germany, reductions of working hours have always been taking place, thus contractual working hours sank by 1.5 hours since 1970 and real working hours per week even sank by 4 hours [28].

The only serious problem to be resolved in this context is how the social security system can be financed without amendments. In reducing working hours, dynamic-forces of a special kind might appear when more work is transferred to the sector of the underground economy (neighbourly help, moonlightling, do-it-yourself); thus payments into the social insurance system diminish. It should be worthwhile to think about whether a part of the consumption and sales taxes on materials used in the underground economy should be taken for the financing of the social security system, because in this sector the wage cannot be drawn upon for financing the social security system. If we succeed in resolving this financing problem, then illicit work could give a fresh competitive impetus to new forms of production.

Footnotes:

(1) Source: Inst.   der Deutschen Wirtschaft (Ed.):
     Zahlen zur Wirtschaftl. Entwicklung der Bundesrepu-
     blik Deutschland, Köln, 1983.

(2) Source: Statist. Bundesamt (Ed.): Wirtschaft u.
     Statistik, 12/1983, Stuttgart, Mainz, 1983, page
     840 and page 860.

(3) We do not include in this discussion the problem of
     foreign workers.

(4) Compare Hof, B.: Arbeitszeitverkürzung - ein Mittel
     der Beschäftigungspolitik? Beiträge zur Wirt-
     schafts- u. Sozialpolitik, Inst. der Deutschen
     Wirtschaft Köln, 1979 and Hof, B.: Arbeitszeitver-
     kürzung - ein Mittel der Beschäftigungspolitik? in:
     Vilmar, F.: Arbeitszeitverkürzung - ein Weg zur
     Vollbeschäftigung?, Opladen, 1983, page 149-174.

(5) Compare Schulz, K.D.: Varianten der Arbeitszeitver-
     kürzung und   ihre Effizienz, in: Beiträge zur
     Arbeitsmarkt- und Berufsforschung, Forschungspreis
     1978 der Bundesanstalt für Arbeit, Stuttgart,
     Nürnberg, 1978, page 191-256.

(6) Compare Terriet, B.: Kasuistik ausgewählter Ansätze
     einer flexiblen Arbeitszeitordnung, in: Mitteilun-
     gen aus der Arbeitsmarkt- und Berufsforschung,
     Stuttgart, Nürnberg, 1979, page 189-299.

(7) Sept. 1982, see table 1 in annex

(8) Sept. 1982, see table 2 in annex

(9) These are persons without any professional experi-
     ence up to now, without indication of economic
     class and unemployed who have not worked for 6
     months and longer.

(10) Sept. 1982, see table 3 in annex

(11) Sept. 1982, see Amtliche Nachrichten der Bundesan-
     stalt für Arbeit, 31. Jahrgang, Nr. 3, 1983, page
     290.

(12) see table 4 in annex

(13) The problem of optimum size of an enterprise in
     connection with working hours should be resolved
     first.

(14) Hayek, Fr.A.v.: Individualismus und Wirtschaftsord-
     nung, Zürich, 1952, page 109.

(15)   Hacker, J.: Beeinflußmöglichkeiten der Arbeitslo-
       sigkeit in der Bundesrepublik Deutschland durch
       Senkung des Arbeitsvolumens, in: Beiträge zur
       Arbeitsmarkt- und Berufsforschung, Forschungspreis
       1978 der Bundesanstalt für Arbeit, page 175-219.

(16)   see Statistisches Bundesamt (Ed.): Wirtschaft u.
       Statistik 7/83, Stuttgart, Mainz, 1983, page
       534-544

(17)   see table 5 in annex

(18)   Differences in growth between branches are reveal-
       ed, for example in the index of industrial net
       production, which in 1982 (1980 = 100) is 91.4 for
       the shoe manufacturing industry, and 115.8 for the
       office machine and computer manufacturing branch.
       See Statistisches Bundesamt (Ed.): Wirtschaft u.
       Statistik 12/83, Stuttgart, Mainz, 1983, page 856.

(19)   Compare Statistisches Bundesamt (Ed.): Wirtschaft
       u. Statistik 7/83, Stuttgart, Mainz, 1983, page 541
       following and Vorkötter, Uwe: Auswirkungen einer
       Verkürzung der Wochenarbeitszeit auf die Nachfrage
       der Unternehmen nach Arbeitskräften, Frankfurt,
       Bern, 1982, page 110 following.

(20)   Source: Statistisches Bundesamt (Ed.): Wirtschaft
       u. Statistik 7/83, Stuttgart, Mainz, 1983, page 540
       following.

(21)   Geometrical degressive rate of depreciation for a
       service life of 4 years were in Germany: 1958
       -1960: 25 %; 1960-1977: 20 %, 1977-1981: 25 % and
       since 29.7.1981: 30 %, Source: Statistisches
       Bundesamt (Ed.): Wirtschaft u. Statistik 12/83,
       Stuttgart, Mainz, 1983, page 922.

(22)   In this way, average costs for a working place were
       30.000 DM in the shoe manufacturing industry,
       190.000 DM in the car construction branch and
       1.550.000 DM in the mineral oil industry! See
       Uhlmann, L.: Was kostet ein Arbeitsplatz? Das
       Verhältnis von Arbeitseinsatz und Kapitaleinsatz in
       der Industrie, Ifo-Schnelldienst, Nr. 33, 1979,
       page 585-586.

(23)   Compare Kunz, D. / Müller, O.G.: Produktivitäts-
       orientierte Arbeitszeitverkürzung als beschäfti-
       gungspolitisches Instrument, in: Mitteilungen aus
       der Arbeitsmarkt- und Berufsforschung, 10. Jg., Nr.
       4, 1977, page 494-505.

(24)   Hansen, Alvin H.: Keynes' ökonomische Lehren,
       Villingen, 1959, page 27.

(25) see Statistisches Bundesamt (Ed.): Wirtschaft u.
      Statistik 12/83, Stuttgart, Mainz, 1983, und
      Institut der Deutschen Wirtschaft (Ed.): Zahlen zur
      wirtschaftlichen Entwicklung der Bundesrepublik
      Deutschland, Köln, 1983.

(26) Statistisches Bundesamt (Ed.): Wirtschaft u. Sta-
      tistik 9/83, Stuttgart, Mainz, 1982, page 684.

(27) Jahresgutachten des Sachverständigenrates zur Be-
      gutachtung der gesamtwirtschaftlichen Entwicklung
      1983/84, Bundestagsdrucksache 10/669, page 143.

(28) Institut der deutschen Wirtschaft (Ed.): Zahlen zur
      wirtschaftlichen Entwicklung der Bundesrepublik
      Deutschland, Köln, 1983.

ANNEX

Table 1: Unemployed Persons and Vacant Positions in the Federal States in September 1982

Federal State	Unemployed Persons	Vacant jobs	Unemployed Persons per Vacancy
Sleswig-Holstein and Hamburg	142 496	5 318	26,8
Lower Saxony and Bremen	283 718	7 952	35,7
North-Rhine-Westphalia	581 092	18 318	31,7
Hesse	138 676	7 465	18,6
Rhineland-Palatinate and Saarland	137 278	5 898	23,3
Baden-Württemberg	185 692	15 798	11,8
Bavaria	270 922	17 052	15,9
Berlin	68 764	3 276	21,0

Source: Amtliche Nachrichten der Bundesanstalt für Arbeit, 31. Jg. Nr. 3, 1983, page 326 and page 361

Table 2: Unemployed Persons and Vacant Positions by Sectors in September 1982

Sector	Unemployed Persons	Vacancies	Unemployed Persons per Vacancy
Agriculture, Foresty & Fisheries	22 694	2 004	11,3
Energy supply, Water, Mining	14 306	283	50,6
Manufacturing	528 234	21 870	24,2
Construction	160 164	8 883	18,0
Distribution	235 682	11 136	21,2
Transport and Communication	48 018	2 185	22,0
Credit Institutions and Insurances	21 482	3 192	6,7
Other Services	260 366	23 236	11,2
Private Households and other Organizations	22 400	3 177	7,1
Governmental Units and Social Insurances 1)	68 756	4 371	15,7
Others	436 536	740	589,9

1) Unemployed persons without previous occupation, unspecified cases and unemployed persons who had interrupted their occupation for six months and more

Source: Amtliche Nachrichten der Bundesanstalt für Arbeit, 31. Jg., Nr. 3, 1983, page 324/325 and page 359/360

Table 3: Unemployed Persons and vacant jobs by the Professional Position and Professional Qualifications

Professional Position Professional Qualifications	End of September 1982			
	Unemployed Persons		Vacant Positions	
	absolute	%	absolute	%
	Cardinal numbers			
All workers	1,207,890	66.4	43,034	53.1
Skilled workers	317,848	17.5	25,544	31.5
Unskilled workers	890,042	48.9	17,490	21.6
Employees altogether	610,748	33.6	38,043	46.9
Employees with high qualifications	387,852	21.3	29,886	36.9
Employees with simple qualifications	222,896	12.3	8,157	10.1
Total	1,818,638	100	81,077	100
with professional qualifications	705,700	38.8	55,430	68.4
without professional qualifications	1,112,938	61.2	26,647	31.6
	Changes over previous year			
All workers	+ 393,856	+48.4	-59,074	-57.0
Skilled workers	+ 165,600	+74.4	-30,428	-54.4
Unskilled workers	+ 258,256	+40.9	-28,646	-62.1
All Employees	+ 168,386	+38.1	-36,135	-48.7
Employees with high qualifications	+ 105,746	+37.5	-28,781	-49.1
Employees with simple qualifications	+ 62,640	+39.1	- 7,354	-47.4
Total	+ 562,242	-44.8	-95,209	-54.0
with professional qualifications	+ 241,346	+52.0	-59,209	-51.6
without professional qualifications	+ 320,896	+40.5	-36,000	-58.4

Source: Amtliche Nachrichten der Bundesanstalt für Arbeit, 31. Jg., Nr. 3, 1983, page 159

Table 4: Unemployment Rates in the Federal Republic of Germany in several Years

	Unemployment Rate [1]											
	Sept. 1982	Sept. 1981	Sept. 1980	May 1980	Sept. 1979	May 1979	Sept. 1978	May 1978	Sept. 1977	May 1977	Sept. 1976	May 1976
	1	2	3	4	5	6	7	8	9	10	11	12
All Unemployed Persons	7.5	5.4	3.5	3.3	3.2	3.4	3.8	4.0	4.0	4.2	3.9	4.2
Males	6.6	4.3	2.6	2.5	2.2	2.4	2.7	3.1	3.0	3.3	3.0	3.5
Females	8.8	7.1	5.1	4.7	4.8	4.9	5.5	5.6	5.7	5.7	5.4	5.4
Foreigners	12.3	8.5	4.8	5.3	3.9	4.4	4.6	5.3	4.3	4.7	3.8	4.8
Full-Time Unemployed												
Persons	7.4	5.1	3.3	3.0	2.9	3.0	3.5	3.7	3.7	3.8	3.6	3.9
Males	6.7	4.3	2.6	2.5	2.2	2.4	2.8	3.2	3.0	3.3	3.1	3.5
Females	9.2	7.0	4.8	4.2	4.4	4.3	5.0	4.9	5.2	5.0	4.8	4.7
Employees	4.9	3.7	2.7	2.5	2.6	2.6	3.1	3.0	3.4	3.4	3.5	3.3
Males	3.0	2.1	1.5	1.4	1.4	1.4	1.6	1.7	2.0	2.1	2.3	2.2
Females	6.9	5.5	4.0	3.7	3.9	3.9	4.6	4.5	5.0	4.9	4.9	4.6
Other professionals (Workers)	10.0	7.1	4.4	4.1	3.8	4.1	4.5	4.9	4.6	4.9	4.3	5.0
Males	9.2	5.9	3.4	3.2	2.8	3.1	3.5	4.1	3.7	4.1	3.6	4.4
Females	12.2	10.0	6.9	6.4	6.2	6.6	6.8	7.0	6.8	6.9	6.2	6.6
Age												
under 20 years	9.1	5.9	3.5	2.5	3.1	2.6	4.4	3.6	5.0	4.1	4.6	3.8
20-25 years	11.5	8.5	5.1	4.5	4.5	4.6	5.8	5.9	6.2	6.3	6.0	6.2
25-30 years	9.8	7.0	4.4	4.2	3.9	4.3	4.8	5.2	5.2	5.4	5.3	5.7
30-35 years	7.4	5.6	3.4	3.3	2.9	3.2	3.4	3.8	3.5	3.8	3.2	3.7
35-40 years	5.8	3.3	2.3	2.2	2.1	2.4	2.6	2.9	2.9	3.2	2.9	3.3
40-45 years	4.9	3.6	2.3	2.4	2.1	2.4	2.8	3.0	3.0	3.3	2.9	3.4
45-50 years	5.2	3.7	2.4	2.4	2.2	2.4	2.6	2.9	2.7	3.1	2.9	3.3
50-55 years	5.2	3.9	2.9	2.9	2.8	3.0	3.2	3.4	3.2	3.4	3.2	3.5
55-60 years	7.8	6.6	5.5	5.7	5.7	5.7	5.6	5.6	5.6	5.5	5.2	5.2
60-65 years	10.7	11.9	9.1	7.3	6.5	6.6	5.3	5.7	4.8	5.3	5.1	5.7

1) In relation to the dependent employed persons (without soldiers) by the Microcensus; Foreigners in relation to the foreignemployees

Source: Amtliche Nachrichten der Bundesanstalt für Arbeit, 31. Jg., Nr. 3, 1983, page 270

Table 5: Remuneration for working performance and additional personnel expenditures per employed person in selected manufacturing sectors

Firms with 10 employees and more

Firms with ... to ... employees / Sector	Remuneration for working performance per employees (DM)				Increase (%) 1975/1972	1978/1975	1981/1978	1981/1972	Additional personnel expenditures per employee (DM)				Increase (%) 1975/1972	1978/1975	1981/1978	1981/1972
	1972	1975	1978	1981					1972	1975	1978	1981				
Production	14 737	18 776	22 603	26 630	27.4	20.4	17.8	80.7	8 191	12 329	15 840	20 099	50.5	28.5	26.9	145.4
10 - 49	14 119	17 090	20 285	23 426	21.0	18.7	15.5	65.9	5 795	8 571	11 891	14 715	47.9	38.7	23.7	153.9
50 - 99	14 258	17 855	20 614	24 697	25.2	15.5	19.8	73.2	6 516	9 533	12 444	15 906	46.3	30.5	27.8	144.1
100 - 199	14 371	17 733	21 242	25 098	23.4	18.2	18.2	74.6	6 840	9 847	13 212	16 639	44.0	34.2	25.9	143.3
200 - 499	14 536	18 233	21 817	25 535	25.4	19.7	17.0	75.7	7 442	10 594	13 980	17 548	42.4	32.0	25.5	135.8
500 - 999	14 004	18 560	22 331	26 392	27.1	20.3	18.2	80.7	7 894	11 985	15 224	19 066	51.8	27.0	25.2	141.5
1 000 and more	15 182	19 886	24 341	28 909	31.0	22.4	18.8	90.4	9 791	15 121	19 058	24 665	54.4	26.0	29.4	151.9
Special Industries:																
Shoe Manufacturing Industry	10 930	13 527	16 391	18 643	23.8	21.2	13.7	70.6	5 059	6 859	9 374	11 119	35.6	36.7	18.6	119.8
Mineral-Oil Ind.	20 412	27 896	35 617	41 496	36.7	27.7	16.5	103.3	13 135	22 606	31 109	39 349	72.1	37.6	26.5	199.6
Office Machines and Computer Manufacturing Industry	17 535	24 379	32 110	38 275	39.0	31.7	19.2	118.3	10 707	17 762	25 532	36 674	65.9	43.7	43.6	242.5

Source: Statistisches Bundesamt (Ed.): Wirtschaft und Statistik 7/83, Stuttgart, Mainz, 1983, page 538

Bm 18

The Impact of Investment for Increased Efficiency on Employment

Bernhard Külp

There is a currently public debate whether technological unemployment accounts for a major share of the current unemployment rate. Labor unions and others claim that investment for increased efficiency destroys jobs and thus contributes to unemployment, while the Council of Economic Advisors declares rationalization to be a necessary condition for maintaining the international competitiveness of the German economy and hence for lowering unemployment in the long run.

This controversy is almost as old as modern economics. During any period of economic crisis (especially in the 1880's and during the Great Depression) there have been proponents of the technological unemployment hypothesis (we may call it the "lay-off hypothesis"), and those who claimed that rationalization would create enough jobs in other parts of the economy to more than outweigh the losses in directly affected industries (the "compensation hypothesis").

At the outset, a definition of rationalization or investment for increased efficiency (taken to be synonymous terms) seems to be in order. Investment for increased efficiency will be understood as any investment that increases the productivity through technical progress or through simple capital-intensification (i.e. substitution along a given isoquante). Empirically, the two tend to appear in common anyway.

As a first step we will have a look at the data to get a preliminary impression of the validity of the lay-off hypothesis (see Diagram 1 in the Appendix). A comparison

of the statistics on the development of the unemployment
rate and the rate of productivity growth for the Federal
Republic of Germany shows no positive correlation between
the two series, they rather indicate an inverse relationship. The rate of growth of labor productivity was
especially high during years of overemployment, while
high unemployment rates in the last years went along with
slow productivity growth.

An analysis of the causes of unemployment should start
with the distinction between "Keynesian" and "classical"
unemployment. In a world where Say's Theorem holds, and
all equilibrating mechanisms function without friction,
long-run unemployment cannot exist; no matter what kind
of data changes lead to temporary lay-offs or dismissals,
the forces of the market are capable of restoring
equilibrium and full employment. Only when the equilibrating mechanisms either in the labor market or in other
markets are disturbed, can there be any meaning to the
question whether the lay-off or the compensating effects
of rationalization dominates. Now the market mechanism
can be disturbed in two ways: Either nominal or real
wages may not respond sufficiently to changes in data, or
labor market participiants may not react elastically
enough to restore full employment. Unemployment is said
to be classical when the ultimate cause for its
maintainance is above-equilibrium real wages, it is said
to be Keynesian when it is related to excess supply in
the goods market.

Diagram 2 in the Appendix shows the Keynesian case.
Consumption is a function of income only and investment
is taken to be autonomous. The fourth quadrant shows the
usual macroeconomic production function. Prices are
assumed to be inflexible in the sense that - although
price variations may occur - the latter are determined by
political forces and not by conditions of disequilibrium.
For the behavior of firms it is assumed that reductions
in the real wage will lead to an increased demand for

labor as long as the firms face no restrictions on the goods market.The lay-off and the compensating effects of investment for increased efficiency can now be analyzed in the framework of this model. On the one hand, rationalization shifts the production function to the right, meaning that any given output can now be produced with less labor, i.e. the increase in labor productivity determines the magnitude of the lay-off effect. The compensation effect depends on the value of three factors: The "investment factor" shows the amount of investment necessary to carry through the rationalization just described. Secondly, the compensation effect is determined by the Keynesian multiplier, which is equal to the reciprocal of the saving rate, assuming a closed economy and no government activity. The third factor is the reciprocal of the elasticity of production with respect to labor indicating by which amount employment will rise, when GNP rises by one per cent. The compensation effect is then defined as the product of the "investment factor", the multiplier and the reciprocal of the elasticity of production with respect to labor. Although the net effect on employment can only be determined empirically, under realistic assumptions concerning the determinants of the compensation effect, the latter will be in general much greater than the lay-off effect.

The last paragraph summarizes the short-run effects of rationalization. Kromphardt has insisted, however, that the compensating effect is of a one-time nature, while the lay-off effect lasts indefinitely. Rationalization will increase labor productivity once and for all, whereas the additional investment occurs in just one period. Thus, no matter which effect is larger in magnitude in the short run, the lay-off effect will eventually dominate unless the increased rate of invest-ment is maintained.

Now modern growth theory has shown that there exists

indeed a rate of growth of investment that will ensure
equilibrium over time. Although it has to be admitted
that post-keynesian growth theory is primarily concerned
with investment for increased capacity, with a given
technology and labor productivity, its basic equilibrium
condition can be modified to allow an analysis of the
kind of investment we are presently dealing with. We
begin with the Keynesian equilibrium condition:

$$I = S$$

Making use of the identity:

$$I = dk/dY \cdot dY$$

and of the savings function:

$$S = s \cdot Y,$$

we can write:

$$dY/Y = s/(dK/dY).$$

Assuming a constant capital coefficient (for a given
point in time), the following substitution is permiss-
ible:

$$dK/dY = K/Y = K/A \cdot A/Y = k/A : Y/A = kappa/pi$$

where kappa denotes capital-intensity and pi the value of
labor productivity. Substituting this expression for the
capital coefficient into the above equation we obtain:

$$dY/Y = s \cdot pi/kappa.$$

The crucial point for our problem turns out to be the
question in which relation pi and kappa will develop

through time.

If the assumption of modern growth theory, that in the
long run technical progress is Harrod-neutral, is
realistic, both magnitudes (rates of growth of capital-intensity and of labor productivity) are ex defi-
nitione equal. In this case the equilibrium condition
remains unchanged, full employment can be maintained even
with permanent rationalization. Even if technical progress is non-neutral, it seems likely that mechanization
proceeds at a faster pace than labor-saving innovation.
In this case full employment can be maintained even with
slower growth rates. In addition, we may note that
Keynesian growth theory denies the functioning of market
mechanisms even in the long run. Only under this
assumption does a constant rate of saving and a
capital-intensity which does not respond to changes in
relative factor prices seem acceptable. Conversely, under
the assumptions of neo-classical growth theory, an excess
supply leads - via a reduction in the interest rate - to
a fall in the rate of saving and to an increase in the
rate of investment, thereby reducing the existing
disequilibrium. Furthermore, the change in relative
factor prices (the interest rate falls in relation to the
wage rate) causes a rise in the capital intensity further
reducing the disequilibrium.
We can summarize these considerations as follows: Only
when the extreme conditions of post-keynesian growth
theory hold, that is,
- the rate of saving is constant and interest-inelastic
- the capital-intensity does not react to changes in
  relative factor prices,
- the rate of growth of labor productivity is higher than
  that of capital-intensity,
only then can investment for increased efficiency lead to
unemployment in the long run also. According to the
knife-edge parable, disequilibrium will in this case even
be self-reinforcing.

Up to this point our analysis was confined to the case of a Keynesian world, where unemployment is caused by a deficiency in aggregate demand. Many economists, however, see the main reason for contemporary unemployment not in a lack of demand, but in real wages that are too high to be consistent with a clearing of the labor market. If this view is correct, the effects of rationalization are quite different from those we analyzed so far.

The relationship between rationalization and employment in this case can be understood quite easily if we visualize a standard demand-supply diagram for the labor market with excess supply because of a real wage rate that is above the equilibrium rate. Investment for increased efficiency will shift the marginal productivity of labor curve, mirrored in the labor demand curve, upwards, and will thus tend to increase employment. The ratio of revenue to costs has improved for firms, giving them an incentive to extend production and hire additional workers. A possible fall in demand for consumption goods will be compensated by increased investment demand assuming that the classical interest-rate mechanism works efficiently. Rationalization thus appears to be a necessary condition for increasing employment, if conditions of classical unemployment prevail. Difficulties with this scenario may occur, however, if labor unions respond to the increase in productivity by demanding a further rise in wages, and if a restrictive monetary policy does not allow the firms to shift these costs on to the consumers through higher prices.

Conclusion

Investment for increased efficiency may lead to technological unemployment if the conditions of the Keynesian model prevail in reality, i.e. in the presence of permanently deficient aggregate demand. In this case, the willingness of firms to invest might be too low to guarantee the absorption of laid-off workers. Since this problem is absent under classical conditions, what might appear to be technological unemployment, can actually only be the result of two quite different forces: a wage policy pursued by labor unions that keeps nominal wages above their equilibrium level in combination with a restrictive monetary policy that does not allow cost pushes to be absorbed in prices. Ceteris paribus, however, rationalization tends to increase employment in the classical model.

Appendix

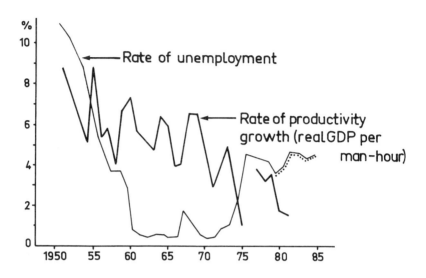

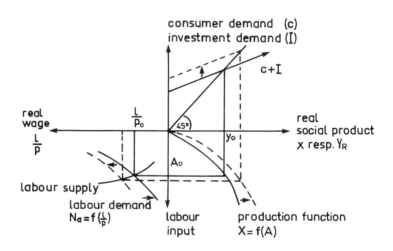

Fixed Investment in a Time of Rapid Technological Change and its Effect on Employment and Productivity

Takashi Matsugi

I Introduction

Fixed investment in the 1960s contributed much to Japan's rapid economic growth, creating lots of job opportunities and strenghthening Japan's competitiveness in the world market. Fiscal policy played an important role in stimulating investment in plant and equipment. During the 1970s, more emphasis was put on environmental considerations rather than on productivity, and after the oil shock in 1973 attempts to save energy also affected investment in a different way.

In recent years, advanced technology in the field of microelectronics has been developing, and arguments have been made concerning its effects on employment, reflecting basically two different positions. Some people say that it is inevitable that unemployment will be increased by the introduction of robots. Others point out the possibility that new jobs will be created, such as jobs teaching computer programming and preparing software in the work-shop. Empirical surveys were made to clarify what the real effects are, both on the national and the regional level. It is generally agreed that new technologies are mostly introduced in order to save on labor input, but that the labor saved is transferred to other positions in the company, giving rise to no dismissals up to today. Slight effects on labor demand have been observed for those newly graduated from highschools and universities.

In this paper those topics will be selected that characterize macro-economic investment behavior in Japan, with policy measures to stimulate fixed investment included as

far as they are relevant. At the same time, special
emphasis will be put on the effects of recent technological changes on employment and productivity with reference
to the results of certain surveys.

II Characteristics of Japanese Fixed Investment in the 1960s and 1970s

II-1 Development of the relative share in GNP and its rate of increase

The relative share of fixed investment in plant and
equipment in the gross national product shows fluctuations according to the stage in the business cycle, as
seen in Figure 1. As for long term development, however,
an upward trend can be observed in the 1960s, and the
share in real terms rose from 14.0 % in 1960, attaining a
peak of 19.5 % in 1970. It remained at around 17 to 19
per cent for some years and then dropped to 15.1 % in
1977, due to the first Oil Shock. A slight recovery has
been recorded in recent shares. The rates of increase in
fixed investment fluctuate more remarkably, as is shown
in Figure 2, in which there are four phases of negative
growth rates during depressions.

Compared with other developed countries, fixed investment
in the private sector in Japan maintains higher relative
shares in GNP. The reasons for this are: (1) the rapid
speed of adjustments to fill the gaps between desired and
actual levels of capital stock, (2) the high profit rate
to be expected in the future, (3) higher savings ratio in
the household sector. The direct effects of the higher
rate of capital formation appear as an increase in the
capital-labor ratio and consequently in labor productivity.

This favorable causation worked less effectively in the
1970s due to two major changes in the economic environ-

Figure 1

Relative Shares of Fixed Investment in GNP.

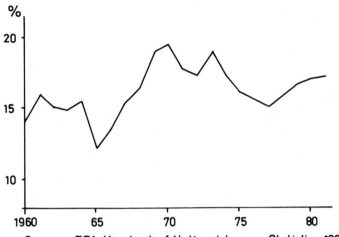

Source : EPA, Yearbook of National Income Statistics, 1983.
(Figure 1 and Figure 2)

Figure 2

Annual Rate of Increase in Fixed Investment.

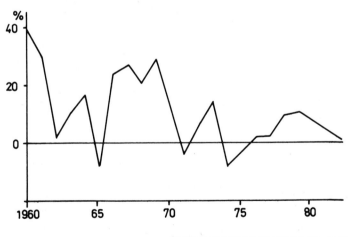

Design: Matsugi
Graphicdesign: IFEP Freiburg i. Br. Kö 87.2

78

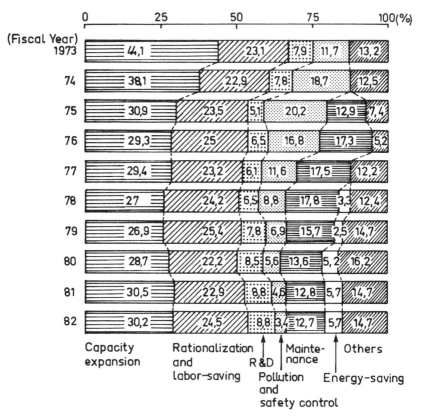

Figure 3

Changing Patterns in Type of Fixed Investment
(Large Firms in Manufacturing).

Source: Japan Development Bank, Survey of Business Spending Plans,
(Surveys were conducted in August in 1973-81 and in February
in 1982)
Capital spendings were divided in terms of their objectives.

Figure 4

Explanations for Increasing Labor- and Energy Saving Investment.

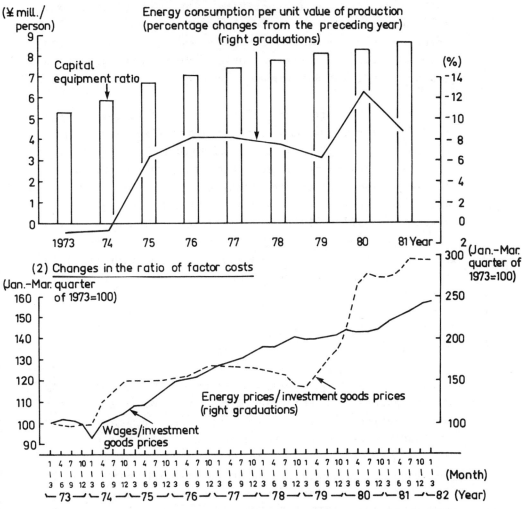

(1) Changes in the capital equipment ratio and energy consumption per unit value of production (manufacturing)

(2) Changes in the ratio of factor costs

Notes:
1. Sources: EPA, Report on National Accounts and Statistics on Business Capital Stock; PMO, Labor Force Survey; MOL, Monthly Labor Survey; BOJ, Price Index Annual Report; MITI, Industrial Statistics; The Institute of Energy Economics, Energy Balance Sheet
2. Capital equipment ratio: Capital stock (averages of those outstanding at the start and the close of terms)/number of employees; Energy consumption per unit value of production; Energy consumption/real value of production. The rate of growth in 1981 was computed by dividing the volume of energy shipments made to the manufacturing industry (the volumes of heavy oil, light oil, kerosene, naphtha, LPG, LNG, coal and electric power were translated into calories) by relevant production indexes.
3. Investment goods prices are deflators of private equipment, wages are based on the regular compensations of manufacturing workers (seasonally adjusted), and energy prices are based on the wholesale prices of fuels and electric power.
Cited from EPA, Economic Survey of Japan 1981/1982, 1982.

| Design: Matsugi |
| Graphicdesign: IFEP Freiburg i. Br. | Kö 87.2 |

ment. The first one was the regulations against environmental damage enacted in 1967 in the Anti-Pollution Law.
A part of new equipment investment was merely to reduce
smoke emission, wastes and dirty water, and contributed
nothing to raising productivity. The second change was
the upsurge in the price for crude oil in 1973.
Enterprises tried to save energy and invested much in
energy saving equipment, which merely replaced old
equipment and did not increase production.

Investment to protect the environment and to save energy
accounted for a sizeable part of total fixed investment.
Evidence for this is supplied by Figure 3, in which the
ratio of investment in pollution and safety control to
the total amounted to more than ten per cent from 1973 to
1977, with an increase in the portion for energy saving
investment since 1978. In addition, Figure 4 gives
information on the relative prices for factors of
production and the energy-capital relation after the 1973
oil crisis made it more profitable to invest in energy
saving equipment.

II-2 Advantageous tax policy to stimulate fixed invest-
      ment

Japanese fixed investment was supported by fiscal policy
in the process of rapid economic growth. Measures for the
modernization of capital equipment have a long history
and contributed much to the economic development of Japan
in the post-war period. One of them is the measure for
the special depreciation of modernization equipment in
important industries. It was initiated in 1952 and
abolished in 1976. This measure allowed firms to
depreciate the value of newly installed machines by 50 %
in the first year, if they were acquired for the purpose
of modernizing the production facilities of the firms.
The special depreciation ratio was lowered later to one
fourth in 1973, 16 % in 1974 and then 8 % in 1975. The
industries covered by this policy were numerous: meat and

dairy products, frozen foods, feeds, spinning, weaving, dying, plywood, petro-chemicals, iron and steel, non-ferrous metals, machinery, electronics, automobiles and parts, steel ship, construction, warehouse, ocean transportation and fishery. The numbers of items and the value of the special depreciation at current prices are summarized in Table 1.

The other measure taken in 1978 was intended as an anti-cyclical policy to help the economy recover from a depression after the first Oil Shock. In 1976 fixed investment in the private sector remained at 80 %, the same level as in 1973, while the comparable level for the Federal Republic of Germany was 92 %, and 88 % for the United States. Investment in plant and equipment experienced negative growth rates in the two successive years, 1974 and 1975, as seen in Figure 2, and then increased yet only at a negligible rate, in the following two years. Accordingly, the average age of capital equipment was higher than before (see in Table 2).

The Ministry of International Trade and Industry (MITI) and the Economic Planning Agency (EPA) stood for the opinion advocated in business circles that a new policy measure was required to revitalize the economy by stimulating investment in the private sector. In April 1978, an investment stimulation tax exemption was introduced though only for a period of one year. This showed that the tax exemption was intended as a policy measure to stimulate business activity, and not as a structural policy to directly subsidize depressed industries. The objects affected by this tax exemption were anti-pollution facilities, energy saving facilities, measures to protect workers from accidents, product inspection equipment, electronic computers and machines acquired by small and medium enterprises. The reason for the exclusion of modernization equipment was that the capital stock adjustment would not proceed actively in the unfavorable economic situation at that time. The amount of tax exempted was up to 10 % of the acquired

Table 1. Performance of Special Depreciation Measure for Equipment Modernization: 1952 - 1967, in billion yen

Fiscal Year	Number of items admitted	Special dep. in value	Fiscal Year	Number of items admitted	Special dep. in value
1952	286	6.2	1960	1,948	73.8
1953	426	18.7	1961	2,244	88.4
1954	501	31.4	1962	2,297	129.4
1955	499	20.5	1963	1,805	102.2
1956	620	17.3	1964	1,126	81.5
1957	1,015	44.4	1965	800	110.6
1958	1,103	59.4	1966	502	88.6
1959	1,396	69.7	1967	669	103.6

Source: MITI Publication of Dec. 15, 1973.

Table 2. Structure of Machines by Year after Installation (in %).

Date of investigation	Number of years after installation				Total
	Less than 5	5 to 10	10 to 20	More than 20	
March 1970	30.9	34.1	17.9	17.1	100.0
Dec. 1976	17.8	31.7	35.9	14.6	100.0

Source: Data compiled by MITI.

items, and if the amount surpassed 20 % of tax payments
for the year (i.e. 1978), the rest could be exempted in
the following three years (i.e. till 1981), so far as the
limit of 20 % in each year was not exceeded.

The following effects were to be expected from this
policy: (1) that the postponement of fixed investment be
stopped, (2) that planned investment be carried out at an
earlier date due to the increased profitability and (3)
that the investment-mindedness on the part of the
entrepreneurs be invigorated. In fact, the rates of
increase in investment in plant and equipment in the
private sector were 9.7 % in 1978 and 10.3 % in 1979 in
real terms.

In April 1981 a measure was taken for energy conservation
activity, to be effective for three years, and to help
lessen the energy cost burdens and also to attain stable
economic growth. The tax advantage was selective, either
in the form of a special depreciation rate of 30 % in the
first year, or a corporate tax exemption equivalent in
value to 7 % of investment expenditures. Then in April
1983 another measure, effective for two years, was
adopted to stimulate small and medium size firms to
invest more in plant and equipment. A special depreciation rate of 30 % was allowed for that part of the
investment expenditures which exceeded the average amount
of investment of the firm in question over the past five
years.

III Effects of New Technologies on Productivity and
     Employment

III-1 Effects on productivity

The Japanese economy is widely famed for its productivity, which provides the background for its strong competitiveness in the world market. However, the productivity

fluctuated over time, and differences among industries have also been great. Japan's physical productivity, expressed as the ratio of the production volume index divided by the employment index, dipped below zero at one time after the first Oil Shock in 1973. Mining and manufacturing productivity in the October-December 1982 period dropped 0.5 per cent from the same period a year earlier. The biggest cause of the recent slowdown is that main sectors, such as the steel and chemical sectors, resorted to production cuts and lower operation rates as a response to the protracted recession. In order to cope with the downturn, companies held new employment in check and temporarily laid off excess workers. As a result, the labor input employed in 1982 in the manufacturing sector decreased by 0.6 per cent. The pace of productivity growth decelerated, because the production volume did not increase substantially and the labor volume was not cut sufficiently.

The only exceptional case in the picture described above the fabrication sector, which is classified into general machinery, electrical machinery, tranportation equipment and precision instruments. Table 3 shows the differences in productivity increases by industry in the six year average growth rate for the 1975-1981 period. The highest rate of 14.8 % was realized in electrical machinery, and the second rank was occupied by precision instruments, then followed by tranportation equipment with 8.9 % and general machinery with an 8.5 % increase in productivity. It is true that a productivity increase is dependent on the market conditions, and in 1982 the productivity in machine manufacturing was raised only by 0.7 % on the average, because demand for machines dropped in the recession.

The improved productivity on the part of the machine manufacturers is no doubt connected with the introduction of microelectronic innovations. In the four industrial branches concerned, the ratios of establishments that

Table 3. Comparisons of Productivity Increase and Robotization by Industry.

Industry	Annual rate of productivity increase for 1975-1981	Ratio of robotization
Foodstuff	2.1 %	2.4 %
Textiles	1.6	3.0
Pulp, Paper & Paper Products	3.9	5.8
Chemicals	6.1	7.9
Petroleum, Coal and Related Pr.	- 2.0	0.0
Ceramics, Stone and Clay Products	- 0.4	0.0
Primary Metals	4.2	21.3
Fabricated Metals	3.7	27.1
General Machinery	8.5	52.9
Electrical Machinery	14.8	32.7
Transportation Equipment	8.9	51.9
Precision Instruments	11.4	36.4

Sources: Ministry for Labor, Annual Report on Labor Economy 1983, Statistical Appendix, Table 1-25. Osaka Prefectural Department of Labor, Effects of Microelectronic Innovation on Employment and Related Policy, 1983.

have introduced robots or NC-machines are very high compared with those in other branches (see Table 3). The survey referred to here was done in Osaka Prefecture, but the results obtained from other surveys support the findings in Osaka. According to the survey done by the Ministry for Labor, for example, 74.2 % of the firms for general machinery have installed microelectronic machines, 72.6 % of transportation equipment firms, 71.5 % of electrical machinery firms, 62.2 % of printing and publishing and 68.4 % precision instruments.

The planning of robotization in the near future also prevails in machine manufacturing. Enterprises which have no interest in microelectronic appliances point out that the reason is that they don't have enough orders to make use of robots, or that the production process in their factory is not suitable for more efficient equipment.

III-2 Effects on employment

Many surveys regarding robotization are concerned with its effects on employment. They provide us a wide range of information on this point. The effects on employment assessed as the change in the number of workers before and after the installation of microelectronic machines are different, depending on where we make the evaluation, namely, whether we are interested in the workshop, the establishment or the company.

Firstly, let us consider the change at the workshop where ME machines are newly introduced. A glance at Table 4 proves that as far as the workshop is concerned, more cases of decreasing number of workers are counted than cases where the number of workers has increased after the introduction of this new type of machine. It of course depends on the extent of robotization, as is shown in Table 4. It should be noted that cases of almost no change make up more than half the total cases on the average.

Table 4. Changes in the Number of Workers before and after the Introduction of ME Machines at the Workshop (in %).

| Extent of introduction | Number of workers after the introduction of ME | | | |
	increased	decreased	no worker	almost no change	total
mostly	10.0	48.0	2.2	39.4	100.0
partly	3.9	37.4	1.2	57.5	100.0
average	4.5	38.5	1.3	55.5	100.0

Source: Ministry for Labor, Survey on Effects of Technological Innovation an Labor, 1983.

Table 5. Effects of ME Innovation on Employment Compiled from Several Surveys.

Conductor of survey	Date of survey	period of comparison	Effects on employment		
			increased	decreased	no change
Min. of Labor	Nov. 1982	one year before the survey	4.6	30.1	65.3
Aichi Pref.	Sept. 1982	from Dec. 1977 to Sept. 1982	48.6	25.0	26.4
Aichi Pref.	Oct. 1982	before and after introduction	17.4	8.3	74.2
Nagano Pref.	Aug. 1982	before and after introduction	8.5	12.5	70.6
Kanagawa Pref.	June 1982	from Apr. 1978 to Apr. 1982	54.0	35.9	10.1
Osaka Pref.	Oct. 1982	from Oct. 1979 to Oct. 1982	43.1	25.2	31.7
Hyogo Pref.	Oct. 1982	before and after introduction	7.4	34.0	58.6

Source: T. Matsugi, Employment Problems in the Time of Microelectronics, in: Chubu Region Development Research Quarterly, March 1984.

Secondly, as for the total effects on the establishments in question, the results from several important surveys are summarized in Table 5.

Effects on employment depend on the length of the period investigated before and after the introduction of ME machines. If the comparison is made in a short time span, answers of "no change" have a higher share, without being affected by other factors which could influence the number of workers. Factors which tend to increase labor input are numerous: need for qualified operators, programmers, instructors, staffs for maintenance, engineers in the area of research and development, etc..

One of the most important factors is an increase in sales, and in this respect it must be remembered that machine manufacturing, in which the introduction of ME technologies is most active, enjoys increasing sales. Another factor not to be neglected is the work shift system. Though the price of robots is declining, they are still expensive, and mangers necessarily are inclined to introduce two or three shifts in order to operate robots for more hours a day. Robots are suited for shift work because they can be operated with less or no personnel. Table 5 must reflect the influence of such factors, at least in cases where the comparison pertains to longer periods.

Appendix 1: Effects of Robotization on Employment

Classification	Number of establishments surveyed	Number of robots introduced	Number of Workers before	Number of Workers after	Labor saving ratio	Type of adjustment transferred to other place	Type of adjustment newly allocated
	A	B	C	D	1-D/C	E	F
Total	75	1,415	1,287	930	27.7 %	450	93
by number of workers							
1,000 and more	22	1,090	910	687	24.5	252	29
300 to 999	18	135	104	80	23.1	45	21
100 to 299	18	137	193	112	42.0	114	33
30 to 99	17	53	80	5	36.3	39	10
by industry							
Metal products	9	71	70	48	31.4	26	4
General machinery	17	123	91	64	29.7	38	11
Elect. machinery	10	32	147	54	63.3	111	18
Transportation equip.	35	1,130	935	924	22.0	255	49
Precision instrum.	5	59	44	35	20.5	20	11
by type of robot							
manual manipulator	3	28	41	40	2.4	4	3
fixed sequence	29	227	174	109	37.4	90	25
variable sequence	10	32	34	21	38.2	18	5
play-back type	36	1,057	869	707	18.6	210	48
numerical control	16	67	163	51	68.7	124	12

Note: D = C - E + F

Appendix 2
_____

Variables	Initial stage	Hypothetical stage	New stage (after robotization)
Number of workers	N_o	$N_o - \Delta N_r$	$N_i = N_o - \Delta N_r + \Delta N_y$ $= N_o (1 - G_{nr} + G_{ny})$
Volume of production	Y_o	Y_o	$Y_i = Y_o + \Delta Y$ $= Y_o (1 + G_y)$
Labor productivity	$\dfrac{Y_o}{N_o}$	$\dfrac{Y_o}{N_o - \Delta N_r}$	$\dfrac{Y_i}{N_i} = \dfrac{Y_o}{N_o - \Delta N_r}$

(1) $\dfrac{N_i}{N_o} = \dfrac{Y_i}{Y_o} \quad \dfrac{N_o - \Delta N_r}{N_o}$

(2) $G_n = \dfrac{N_i - N_o}{N_o} = (1 + G_y) \; (1 - G_{nr}) - 1$

(3) $G_n = G_y - G_{nr} - G_y G_{nr}$

Segmentation Theories and their Applicability
for the Labor Market
of the Federal Republic of Germany

Rainer Feninger

1. Approaches of the Segmentation Theory
1.1. Theory of the Imperfect Market

According to the idea of perfect competition in the neo-classical models, disequilibria in the labor markets should not occur in reality. If, however, they do occur these disequilibria are considered only temporary since the market mechanism will set in motion a tendency to equilibrium. But long-term disequilibria in the forms of unemployment and disparities in the distribution of incomes can be observed in the labor market. The reasons for this are not seen in the horizontal restrictions of competition as neoclassical theory argues, but rather in vertical limitation of mobility.

Other assumptions of the model are also not fulfilled. For example perfect information is not given: job searchers can be characterized by a lack of knowledge of the supply and demand on the labor market, strengthened by a missing or limited regional mobility and the costs of information. Moreover, it is obvious that both suppliers and demanders have specific preferences.[1]

Special problems on the labor market are a result from the fact that the decisions of those who offer their services are not only determined by economic, but also by social factors. The questions discussed in the labor market theories are therefore often not confined to pure economic areas but extend into the sociological field.

In face of the different market imperfections it seems to be necessary to give up, completely or partially, the relevance of the neoclassical "wage competition" because it can be observed that the labor market leads to incurable inadequate disparities of incomes and disequilibriums on the labor market. For instance disequilibria should lead to a decrease of wages in areas with an excess supply of jobs.

The "negative feed backs" which characterize the neoclassical model can hardly be observed. So it seems to be reasonable to give up the exclusive validity of "wage competition" and the assumption of "negative feed backs" and to move in the direction of a "job competition"[2] and of "positive feed backs".

1.2. "Job Search and Labor Turnover"-Theory

This theoretical approach is relatively close to the basic neoclassic concept, because it does not presume given institutional segments and assumes neoclassical market mechanisms like "wage competition". In this neoclassical model of segmentation[3] a segment is formally defined "if an unemployed person and a job do not meet, and the level of wage is not the reason thereof."[4]

It is not easy to find a separation to the "Dual-Labor Market"-model, since the "weak" mobility as classification criterion for the two segments within the "Dual Labor Market" - model cannot be measured in an "objective" way. This criticism, expressed by the representatives of neoclassical approaches of the segmentation theory[5], is further emphasized by the argument that if consideration would be restricted to two given separated segments some studies on mobility would be neglected.[6]

The basic point of the job search theory is the fact, that jobs are permanently changed and require an extensive searching activity. This theory considers the total labor market. Smooth functioning in the market is mainly inhibited by a lack of information, search problems, as well as costs.

In this theory the economy is compared with a world of islands which represent the different segments of the labor market. It is the task of those who are living on those islands and are searching for jobs, to get informations about the situation on the other islands. Costs, time for searching, and as a consequence unemployment indicate how well the information flows between these segments.

Whether an agreement on a work contract is reached depends on the acceptance of a certain wage. A permanent search and adaptation process, caused on one side by the supply of jobs and the search for jobs on the other side, determines the movements of wages. A significant factor for the influence on the level of wages is the power of negotiation on both sides of the market.

A reorientation away from the approach of the 'Job Search and Labor Turnover'-theories towards the 'Dual-Labor Market'-theory is to be seen in further variables such as qualification, location, sex, etc. which are of importance for the realization of the working relationship. Institutional restrictions are of less importance than in the 'Dual-Labor Market'-theory, and in a long term perspective the emphasis is mainly placed on economic powers.

1.3. "Dual-Labor Market"-Theory

In the following discussion of the approaches of the Segmentation Theory the emphasis is placed on the consideration of the 'Dual-Labor Market'-theory. In this theory the labor market is mainly divided into a primary

and a secondary segment, with the primary segment being
further segmented into a higher and lower part. Jobs of
the primary segment are characterized by high wages and
mainly found in firms and industries with internal
markets.[7] The influence of the unions makes these jobs
secure, the conditions of work and the chances of starting
a career are good. The secondary segment comprises bad
jobs. The Segmentation Theory presumes that the wages in
this part of the labor market are also determined by
political and social factors.[8] Persons who are working in
those jobs do not usually identify themselves with their
job and the firm. Dissatisfaction is the cause for
frequent job changes; this employment also depends
strongly on the economic situation. Typical are also the
high rates of fluctuation and unemployment of employees
with low qualification.[9]

The division in the two segments is explained by a limited
vertical mobility and entrance limitations. A significant
hypothesis of the model is that the limitations which
reduce or even prevent the mobility from one segment to
the other cannot be explained by the neoclassical
theories. For instance, it is observed that also in the
secondary segment, the employees have a high potential of
human capital. The following factors: race, sex, economic
depressions, changes in the economic structure between
industrial branches or regions, are responsible for the
remains in the secondary segment. From this perspective
the most important reason for institutional limitations in
the discussion of the dual market model is discrimination
(especially racial discrimination). But the fact that in
the secondary segment people are employed who possess only
a low level of capability, such as young people, employees
without any education, and women who are searching for
parttime jobs, should not be neglected. The lack of human
capital which leads to unemployment in the secondary
segment and a corresponding (adequate) low level of wages,
is in accordance with the neoclassical argumentation, that
is, the presumption that wages depend on the productivity.

From the Dualists' standpoint those neoclassical arguments are overstressed because highly qualified employees also remain in the secondary segment. That means that the limitations of mobility and entrance are working well.[10]

The reasons for the stability of segmentation are seen in the behavior of the employees in the secondary segment as well as in the structure of production. The mobility of the employees is influenced by their membership to a group, because the demanded qualification for a job is determined by the interrelation of the individual employee and his group.[11]

Also there can be given a production theoretical explanation: jobs that satisfy the criteria of the primary segment as security and continuity are only possible on the basis of a highly industrialized economy. This results in the separation of (mass-)production and management. This corresponds to the distinction between the secondary and lower part of the primary segment on one hand, and the higher part of the primary segment on the other. Because of the heterogenous qualification of the employees the interchangeability between different functional levels becomes highly implausible in big firms. A continuous rise in the status hierarchy from unqualified worker to top manager is very unlikely. In many areas employees with a higher status do not have to have the professional qualification of a lower-ranking employee and vice versa. This is another barrier for mobility between segments.

2.   The Labor Market in the Federal Republic of Germany
2.1. Structure of Production

The structure of production is characterized by big and small firms with typical production methods, which result in various forms of work organisation that involves differences in the structure of employment.[12]   The following statements can be made:

a) The production plants can be divided into a primary area[13] which consists of big firms with more than 1000 employees and a secondary area with small firms with less than 100 employees.

b) In the primary area work conditions are better; that is indicated for instance by higher than average wages (see table 1).

This gap between big and small firms is actually increased by voluntary welfare charges.

A high employment stability can be shown as expressed by the length of time membership to firms (see table 2).

Additionally the percentage of older people is higher in big firms than in small firms.

c) In reference to these results firms which belong to the secondary area show worse conditions according to the criterias above.

2.2. Structure of Employment
2.2.1. Primary Segment

Groups of performance will be arranged according to the primary segment. Groups of performances I, II, III of employees as well as group 1 and 2 of workers (a classification made by 'Statistics Germany') are regarded as important.[14]

Finally, it should be examined if the application of social and cultural features related to the jobs in the primary segment will lead to different statements. Here a sex specific division should be considered (see table 3).

Among the employees, a distinctive division in reference

Table 1: Average payment for work in firms with 50-99 and more than 1000 employees

| | Workers | | Employees |
	hourly wage	yearly wage	yearly salary
<100	4.45	8,357	11,407
>1.000	4.60	8,513	12,524

Source: Ahner, D.: Übersicht 3, p. 145

Table 2: Per cent of the 'instable' (= less than three years of membership to a firm) and the 'stable' (= 15 years and more) in big and small firms

| | Membership to the firm | | | | | |
| | A <3 years | | B ≥15 years | | Relation B : A | |
	workers	employees	workers	employees	workers	employees
<100	39.65	35.82	9.15	12.15	0.23	0.34
>1.000	24.17	25.6	22.68	25.2	0.94	0.98

Source: Ahner, D.: 1978, Übersicht 5, p. 149

Table 3: Distribution of male and female commercial employees on the various levels of hierarchy (in %)

		Performance Group				
		V	IV	III	II	I
1966	women	10.3	55.3	30.1	3.7	0.4
	men	2.9	20.5	48.6	22.3	5.5
1978	women	6.9	47.4	40.0	5.1	0.42
	men	1.67	14.2	49.1	28.0	6.9

Source: Ahner, D.: 1978, Übersicht 23, p. 184; own calculations after: Statistisches Bundesamt: 1982

Table 4: Shares of women in the various groups of performance (workers) in 1966

Performance group	Female workers in		
	3	2	1
<100 workers	25.6	22.3	2.5
Ø of all enterprises	43.9	23.7	2.3
>1.000 workers	54.4	19.0	1.2

Source: Ahner, D.: 1978, Übersicht 27, p. 195

to the occupation of higher and lower performance groups of by women and men can be shown.

According to the number of jobs about 80% of the women belong to the performance group V and about 75% to group IV in 1966 (see table 4).

Women are hardly represented in the primary section. Their portion in big firms is still smaller than in small firms. Although the considered criterias are limited as a base for judgment, it is obvious that this is a primary segment on the labor market. Related to this segment the owners of firms do not only make their decision on criterias such as the qualification of the labor forces.

2.2.2. Secondary Segment

This segment combines performance group IV and V (employees) and 2 and 3 (workers) (see table 5 and table 6).

In the lowest area of work, which is mainly carried out by labor forces without education, a distinctive accumulation of women and foreigners can be shown. With an increasing level of work the percentage of men increases while the percentage of women and foreigners are reduced; the portion of employed women and foreigners are larger in small firms. As a result, a clear influence of the social and cultural component on the professional status can be stated.

For the secondary segment the situation of the foreign workers is of interest. It can be shown that, as theoretically presumed, the fluctuation is extremely high and a strong dependency on the economic situation is given (see table 7).

In the area of employees it is recognized that the arrangement of men and women according to the secondary

Table 5: Distribution of German and foreign workers as well as men and women within the various groups of performance in big and small firms

		Enterprises								
		<50 employees			total			>1.000 employees		
		3	2	1	3	2	1	3	2	1
1966	German workers	8.8	21.2	70.0	12.3	30.6	57.2	12.9	34.5	52.6
1966	Foreign workers	35.0	37.0	28.0	35.0	47.0	18.0	33.0	54.0	13.0
1966	men	13.3	22.5	64.2	11.5	31.2	57.3	8.9	36.6	-54.5
	women	35.4	50.6	14.0	45.0	48.4	6.6	53.4	43.3	3.3
1978	men	10.5	16.6	72.8	9.6	26.4	63.9	7.7	32.3	60.0
	women	36.7	48.0	15.1	49.8	43.5	6.6	52.6	41.9	5.4

Source: Ahner, D.: 1978, p. 212; own calculations after: Statistisches Bundesamt: 1982

Table 6: Shares of german and foreign workers as well as men and women within the various groups of performance in big and small firms

		Enterprises							
		<50 employees				>1.000 employees			
		Germans	Foreigners	men	women	Germans	Foreigners	men	women
1966	3	42.3	57.4	77.8	22.2	66.5	33.5	54.4	45.6
	2	63.0	37.0	80.7	19.3	76.3	23.7	81.0	19.0
	1	88.1	11.9	97.7	2.3	95.3	4.7	98.8	1.2
1978	3			70.4	29.6			69.4	30.6
	2			72.4	27.6			80.5	19.5
	1			97.4	2.6			98.4	1.6

Source: Ahner, D.: 1978, p. 212; own calculations after: Statistisches Bundesamt: 1982

Table 7: Growth rates of GNP, industrial net production and employees

year	GNP	industr. net production	Employees		
			total	industry only	foreigners
1964	6.6	8.6	1.1	0.3	16.7
1965	4.4	5.3	1.4	1.9	24.0
1966	2.5	1.8	0.1	- 0.7	11.2
1967	1.0	- 2.4	- 3.2	- 6.4	- 18.5
1968	9.0	11.8	0.7	0.3	0.5
1969	11.7	13.0	2.8	5.2	34.0

Source: Ahner, D.: 1978, Übersicht 41, p. 224

segment from the above mentioned division into performance
groups does not seem to be possible (see table 8).

With regard to the average time of membership to firms,
men are relatively favored. So the performance group V can
be definitely placed into the secondary segment; in the
performance group IV it is possible that some of the jobs
done by men meet criterias for jobs which must to be
placed into the lower part of the primary segment of the
labor market.

2.3. Synthesis

Both production plants and the structure of employment in
the FRG are heterogenous and so they can be divided into
two areas or segments (see chart 1).

It is clear that for the labor market in the FRG the
condition of an imperfect market must be presumed.
According to these aspects, the picture of a segmented
labor market appears. The inclusion of the structure of
production leads to another division (see chart 2).

It is recognized that mobility exists within the secondary
segment, not only within the areas of big firms and small
firms, but also between them. This confirms the thesis of
the existence of horizontal mobility in the secondary
segment of the labor market in an internal and external
form. This is not valid for the primary segment. Here,
mobility occurs exclusively in form of internal mobility
within big firms and interfirm mobility in small firms.

Vertical mobility from the secondary to the primary
segment appears in a different way. It exists, within
small firms as well as in areas of big firms, which belong
to the secondary segment to the area of small firms.

In both cases a career is only possible in the lower part

Table 8: Average membership and age of employees in low performance group in big and small firms

		<100		all enterprises		>1.000	
		Øemployees	Øage	Øemployees	Øage	Øemployees	Øage
men	V	6.11	37.98	6.59	40.48	8.24	41.0
	IV	7.03	32.25	7.96	34.59	9.11	36.65
	III	8.86	37.49	10.03	38.78	11.41	39.81
women	V	4.87	32.97	4.88	29.14	5.01	36.58
	IV	6.15	27.56	6.49	29.33	7.10	31.41
	III	7.96	28.8	8.58	34.44	10.84	29.19

Source: Ahner, D.: 1978, Übersicht 39, p. 220

Chart 1

Heterogenity of
total production facilities

Structure of Employment

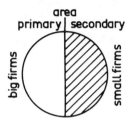

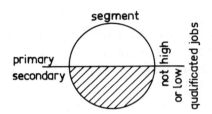

Source: Ahner, D.: 1978, p. 180

Chart 2

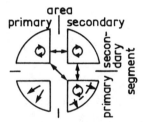

↙ intern mobility

↻ interfirm mobility

⟷ mobility between parts
of the areas

Source: Ahner, D.: 1978, p. 240

Chart 3

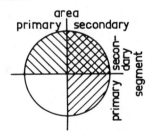

◸ system of intern labor markets ⎱ primary
in big firms ⎰ labor market

◩ separated secondary segment
in big firms

◪ qualificated jobs (specialized) ⎱ secondary
in small firms ⎰ labor market

▨ not and low qualificated jobs
in small firms

Source: Ahner, D.: 1978, p. 233

of the primary segment. A clear vertical limitation of mobility to the primary segment exists, but only in relation to the area of the big firms.

The question as to which arrangement of the two segments for the labor market could result from this consideration, can not be clearly answered. Ahner designed the following division (see chart 3).

The final question is to what extent parts in the primary segment of the structure of employment in the area of small firms would also belong to the primary segment of the labor market.

Notes

1) For example: regional preferences (living place), habits, language barriers; climate on the work place, and factors such as location of the firm, age, sex and origin of the worker.
2) Thurow, L.C.: 1978, p. 118
3) Wachter, M.L.: 1978, p. 155
4) Freiburghaus, D.: 1976, p. 88
5) Wachter, M.L.: 1978, p. 155
6) Andrisani, P.J.: 1973
7) Wachter, M.L.: 1978, p. 141
8) Freiburghaus, D.: 1979, p. 175
9) Freiburghaus, D.: 1979, p. 172
10) Wachter, M.L.: 1978, p. 156
11) Feninger, R.: 1980, p. 116
12) Ahner, D.: 1978, p. 143
13) The following terms of primary and secondary "areas" and "segments" are not identic to use as done in the division in segments of the labor market
14) Ahner, D.: 1978, p. 184

References

AHNER, D. (1978): Arbeitsmarkt und Lohnstruktur. Tübingen.

ANDRISANI, P.J. (1973): An Empirical Analysis of the Dual Labor Market Theory. The Ohio State University, Ph. D. Dissertation.

BOLLE, M. (Ed.) (1976): Arbeitsmarkttheorie und Arbeitsmarktpolitik. Opladen.

CAIN, G.G. (1976): The Challenge of Segmented Labor Market Theories to Orthodox Theory: A Survey. The Journal of Economic Literature, Vol. 14, p. 1215-1257.

FENINGER, R. (1980): Ausbildungserträge. Eine systemtheoretische Wirkungsanalyse. Freiburg.

FREIBURGHAUS, D. (1976): Zentrale Kontroversen der neueren Arbeitsmarkttheorie. In: Bolle, M. (Ed.): Arbeitsmarkttheorie und Arbeitsmarktpolitik. Opladen, p. 71-91.

FREIBURGHAUS, D. (1978): Arbeitsmarktsegmentation - Wissenschaftliche Modeerscheinung oder arbeitsmarkttheoretische Revolution? Discussion Paper Series. International Institute of Management. Berlin.

MILL; J.St. (1849): Principles of Political Economy. Vol. I. London.

SENGENBERGER, W. (1978): Einführung: Die Segmentation des Arbeitsmarktes als politisches und wissenschaftliches Problem. In: Sengenberger, W. (Ed.): Der gespaltene Arbeitsmarkt. Probleme der Arbeitsmarktsegmentation. Frankfurt/New York, p. 15-42.

SENGENBERGER, W. (1979): Zur Dynamik der Arbeitsmarktsegmentierung - mit Thesen zur Struktur und Entwicklung des Arbeitsmarktes in der Bundesrepublik Deutschland. In: Brinkmann, Ch. u.a. (Ed.): Arbeitsmarktsegmentation - Theorie und Therapie im Lichte der empirischen Befunde. Beiträge zur Arbeitsmarkt- und Berufsforschung 33. Nürnberg, p. 1-44.

STATISTISCHES BUNDESAMT (1970): Fachserie M: Preise, Löhne, Wirtschaftsrechnungen, Reihe 17: Gehalts- und Lohnstrukturerhebungen, I. Gewerbliche Wirtschaft und Dienstleistungsbereich, Arbeitsverdienste 1966. Stuttgart/Mainz.

STATISTISCHES BUNDESAMT (1982): Gehalts- und Lohnstrukturerhebung 1978, Fachserie 16, Löhne und Gehälter. Stuttgart/Mainz.

THUROW, L.C. (1972): Education and Economic Equality. Public Interest, Vol. 28, p. 66-81.

THUROW, L.C. (1978): Die Arbeitskräfteschlange und das Modell des Arbeitsplatzwettbewerbs. In: Sengenberger, W. (Ed.): Der gespaltene Arbeitsmarkt. Probleme der Arbeitsmarktsegmentation. Frankfurt/ New York, p. 117-137.

VIETORISZ, T., HARRISON, B. (1973): Labor Market Segmentation: Positive Feedback and Divergent Development. The American Economic Review, Papers and Proceedings, Vol. 63, p. 366-376.

WACHTER, M.L. (1978): Das Konzept des dualen Arbeitsmarktes aus neoklassischer Sicht. In: Sengenberger, W. (Ed.): Der gespaltene Arbeitsmarkt. Probleme der Arbeitsmarktsegmentation. Frankfurt/New York, p. 139-184.

WILLEKE, F. (1956): Arbeitsmarkt. Handwörterbuch der Sozialwissenschaften, Bd. 1, Göttingen, p. 321-332.

Manpower Adjustment Policies
of Firms under Microelectronic Innovation

Masao Toda

I Introduction

The first oil shock of 1973 marked a turning point, after
which fundamental structural changes seem to have been
taking place in the Japanese economy. There was a major
shift in the governmental industrial policy, away from
old-style growthmanship and industrialization, toward the
production of more value-added products using less
energy, resources and labor[1].

Electronics plays a central role in this new era in
Japan's economic history. The introduction of microelectronic devices has produced products of higher quality
(therefore, more valuable) with less labor (thus less
expensively, investment costs in new machinery and
equipment aside). This naturally provides a strong
temptation for enterprises to introduce microelectronics
in an attempt to maximize their profits in a competitive
industry.

As might be anticipated, this 'microelectronic revolution' has been accompanied by sustained declines in
manufacturing employment. Chart 1 shows ratios of
establishments using equipment containing integrated
circuits and the changes in employment. In every industry
a very small fraction (3 to 4 percent on average) of
establishments have increased their employment of workers, while a sizeable number of establishments have
decreased their work force.

However, this does not necessarily mean that such high
numbers of employees were laid off, for two reasons:

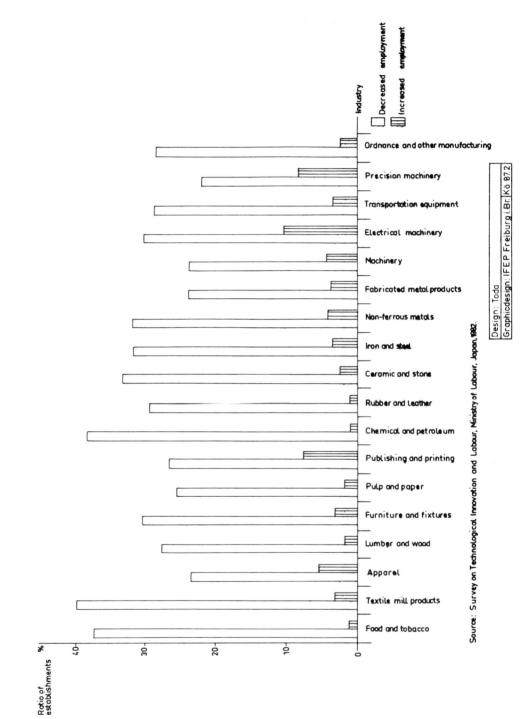

Chart 1

Ratio of establishments using equipment with IC by industry employment changes (1982)

Source: Survey on Technological Innovation and Labour, Ministry of Labour, Japan, 1982.

Design: Toda
Graphicdesign: IFEP Freiburg i.Br.Kö 87.2

First, there are inter-establishment transfers within an enterprise. Under the well-known custom of the 'life-long employment system of Japan, it is very likely that "excess" employees in an establishment A which has suffered from declines in demand for its products will be transferred to another establishment B which is experiencing an upward demand for its line of products. Secondly, although not revealed in Chart 1, more than 40 percent (on the average) of the establishments have apparently managed to maintain their existing level of employment.

How could this be achieved? Some economists, notably Muramatsu, have noted the role of working hours as an adjustment mode between employment size and changes in product demand. Even if the product demand declines, an enterprise can maintain its work force in the short run by cutting the number of working hours instead. Muramatsu's empirical work (1981)[2] has confirmed this hypothesis.

Recent survey findings (1982)[3], contrary to Muramatsu's, hint at the possibility of another important mode of internal adjustment and the necessity of an inquiry into a new area: transfers within an enterprise and retraining of the transferred employees. In contrast to the manipulation of working hours, which is a shortrun method of labor adjustment in relation to product demand, a long-run effect characterizes the intraenterprise mode of adjustment. Once the employees are transferred, they may remain at the new position for their remaining working life.

This paper attempts to show the statistical importance of intraenterprise transfers in Japan's manufacturing industries and to outline the economic logic behind this behavior by the firms. Section II discusses the determinants of the rate of intraenterprises transfer. Enterprise policies for retraining the transferred are

considered in Section III. Section IV concludes the paper
and suggests areas of future research.

II   Intraenterprise Transfers and Retraining of the Transferred

II 1   A Statistical Overview of Intraenterprise Transfers

A recent finding, based on the Ministry of Labor's Survey
on Technological Innovation and Labor, revealed the
short-run nature of working hours adjustments. Ten years
after the first oil shock of 1973, total working hours of
all plants seem to remain very stable, with only less
than 10 percent of the establishments experiencing
shorter hours (Chart 2). This finding indicates that the
working hours during the period from 1970 to 1977, based
on Muramatsu's results, had decreased, but since then
recovered to become stable in 1982. Of course, it is not
very accurate to evaluate the two results based on
different sample surveys.
Even more importantly, working hours fail to show any
noticeable difference between different sizes of establishments using equipment involving IC. It was therefore
decided to discard working hours from a list of probable
elements to determine the effects of microelectronics
innovation on employment behavior of enterprises.

II 2   The Theory of Internal Labor Markets

The series of charts from Chart 3 through 6 suggest
alternative instruments for internal allocation of labor
when a decrease in the work force becomes inescapable
through the introduction of computers and memory chips.
There exists a clear stable positive relationship between
enterprise size and the extent of intraenterprise
transfers.   This   relationship   apparently   has

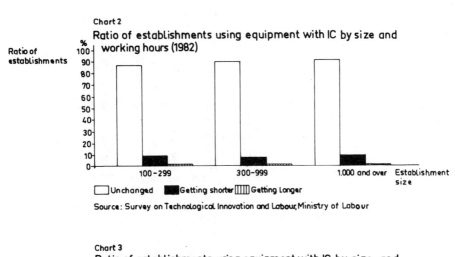

Chart 2

Ratio of establishments using equipment with IC by size and working hours (1982)

Ratio of establishments

%

Establishment size

☐ Unchanged   ■ Getting shorter   ▥ Getting Longer

Source: Survey on Technological Innovation and Labour, Ministry of Labour

Chart 3

Ratio of establishments using equipment with IC by size and way of transfer (1982)

Ratio of establishments

%

Establishment size

▥ Transfer within the same establishment   ▦ Transfer to another establishment within the firm

■ Sent to affiliated company   ☐ Dismissal or inducement to leave employment   ▥ Without any transfer

Source: Survey on Technological Innovation and Labour, Ministry of Labour

Design: Toda	
Graphicdesign: IFEP Freiburg i. Br.	Kö 87.2

116

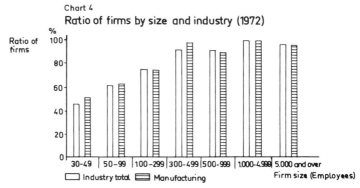

Chart 4
Ratio of firms by size and industry (1972)

Source : Survey on Employment Management, Ministry of Labour, 1972.

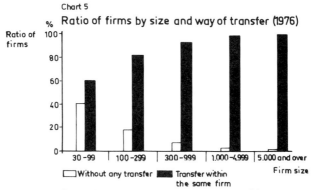

Chart 5
Ratio of firms by size and way of transfer (1976)

Source: Survey on Employment Management, Ministry of Labour, 1976.

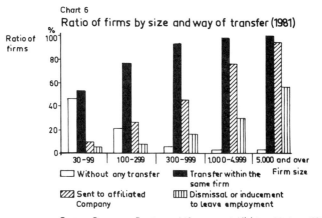

Chart 6
Ratio of firms by size and way of transfer (1981)

Source : Survey on Employment Management, Ministry of Labour, 1981.

Design: Toda
Graphicdesign: IFEP Freiburg i.Br. Kö 87.2

survived the first and second oil shocks in 1973 and 1978, and the recent wave of the electromechanics revolution.

An enterprise facing an allocative problem for its work force usually has five alternative choices: (1) to transfer workers within the same establishment, (2) to transfer them to another establishment within the firm, (3) to send them to an affiliated company, (4) to dismiss or induce them to leave employment, and (5) to do without any transfer. The choices of (1) and (2) consist of an intraenterprise transfer, and those of (3) and (4) belong to an interenterprise transfer.

The literature on internal labor markets pioneered by Doeringer and Piore (1971)[4] provides a basic explanation for the behavior of an enterprise. The economic efficiency of the internal labor market, characterized by skill specificity, on-the-job training, possibilities to rise on the promotion ladder, may be counterbalanced by customary rules designed to increase job security or equitable treatment of the internal labor force.

The employer's interest is to minimize the cost of turnover, which is the sum of the costs of replacement (recruitment, screening, and training) and the cost of termination (severance pay and unemployment insurance). The employer's quest for allocative efficiency is generally modified to accomodate employee interests. The transfer pattern represented in Chart 3 can be easily explained by the aforementioned framework. It involves a net loss of skill if a specifically skilled worker has to be transferred to another establishment, in the same enterprise. It is even more costly if he has to be sent to an affiliated company. The worker is likely to resist this type of transfer because he may have to start a new career very different from the one he had at his former establishment or enterprise, and because it creates difficulties for his family in adjusting to a new environment.

Whether his resistance to the company's orders is
accepted or not depends upon the existence of a
management-union agreement concerning transfers and upon
the strength of a union's bargaining power on this
matter. To avoid confrontation with the union, and to
minimize a turnover cost, an enterprise will refrain from
opting for dimissal or sending an employee to an
affiliated company. This explains why the incidence of
these two types of transfer is so seldom, as shown in
Chart 3 and 6.

II 3   The Nature of Microelectronic Innovation and the
         Induced Changes in Job Content

Charts 3 through 6 also reveal a significant number of
transfers within the same establishment. We now turn to
an explanation of this phenomenon.

Our focus of attention is limited to manufacturing for
two reasons. First, the impact of office automation on
employment may have been felt more greatly in the service
sector, and surveys in this sector have just begun.[5]
Secondly, the manufacturing industry is the mother
industry of microelectronics in the sense that some of
the manufacturing industries use microelectronics in the
production of microelectronic products. It is in this
industry that the substitution of computers for labor is
taking place most vividly.

The introduction of microelectronics has been transfor-
ming the quality of labor and therefore job content in
the production line[6]. Machining center is a multipurpose
numerical control (NC) machine tool that automatically
controls 10 to 20 different tools for precision cutting.
It seems that machines are being used for complicated
tasks, leaving the simpler ones to the workers. This may
even be the case for a supervisory job once the machine

starts doing the job. A skilled operator is nevertheless required. To work with a multipurpose machine for a relatively small quantity of products (one lot varies from just a few to several hundred products), one has to know the properties of the materials and tools and have the know-how for cutting, processing, and treatment of a wider range of products. As the operator of a machine, one has to be able to program its software as is necessitated by the fexible mode of production.

Basic knowledge of cutting, processing, and treating is indispensable even when working with a computer- equipped machine. Therefore, it is unlikely that someone from outside can do a job well, and tasks have to be performed by workers from within an enterprise. However, the operators of those microelectronics also need to maintain them, which requires both basic and advanced training in electric and electronic disciplines. The machines necessitate very simple manual work, too, such as attaching and removing pre-fabricated parts, and replacing tools.

By combining the above NC machines with automatic palette changers and carrier robots, numerous establishments have installed flexible manufacturing systems (FMS). One example, which is typical, is shown in the following Diagram 1.

In this example, after the introduction of FMS, working hours have been changed to a 24-hour work system of one shift with 6 persons (daytime) and one with 3 persons during the night. As a result, productivity has gone up, and eight workers were eliminated from the process.

Diagram 1

Observed changes in process before and after the introduction of flexible manufacturing system

BEFORE

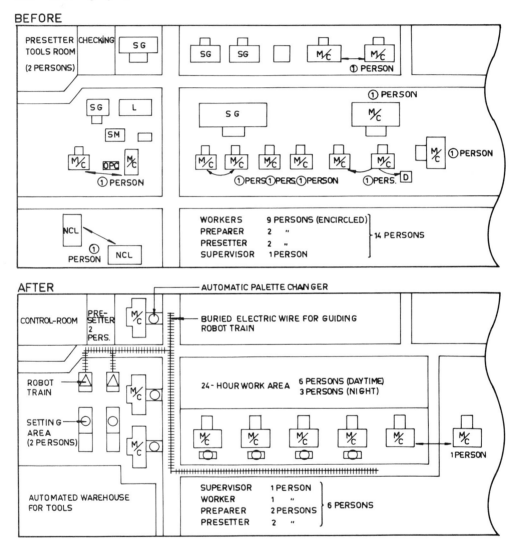

AFTER

Note: SG surface grinder, M/C machining center, L lathe, SM plain milling machine, NCL numerical control turret lathe, OPC automatic palette changer

Source: Osaka Productivity Center ed., _Electromechanics Revolution and Industrial policy_ (Chairman: Prof. Kazuo Koike) 1983, pp. 47-48

Design: Toda	
Graphicdesign: IFEP Freiburg i. Br.	Kö 87.2

II 4   Retraining the Transferred: Patterns Found from
         the Survey on Employment Management

As discussed in the previous section, the advent of a new
technology has created two types of jobs; very simple
manual work easily done even by a part-time employee on
the one hand, and jobs which require high intellectual
calibre supported by skill, especially enterprise-speci-
fic, nurtured during many years of experience at the
enterprise on the other hand. Added to this is the
well-observed fact that an enterprise rarely fires its
prime workers because it fears permanent layoffs will
damage the "company reputation" in the society. In fact,
with no exception, the interviewees of seven companies
have indicated to this author that they think the company
would like to lay off its excess work force if it ever
were to become socially acceptable.

To summarize, an enterprise wishes to trim its labor
force, to increase productivity (this means producing
more output per employee), and to produce more value-
added products (this means producing higher-priced output
per employee), not because it prefers this way, but
becaue it has to do so if it ever wishes to survive the
fierce competition within the industry. In addition, the
enterprise cannot fire its workers. There exists only one
solution to this dilemma: adjusting the number of workers
through intraenterprise transfer, and adapt the transferred through retraining within the enterprise, which is
the main topic of inquiry in this paper.

Information on within-enterprise vocational training is
very limited. A wide number of surveys exist, but their
sample sizes are generally insufficient. The first
comprehensive survey to date, to this author's knowledge,
is the 1977 Survey on Employment Management, conducted by
the Ministry of Labor in Japan. Thus our study starts by
examining this important source of data in order to say

something about transfer-retraining policies of enterprises under technological innovation.

The 1977 Survey on Employment Management

There have been gradual changes which cause an enterprise to adjust its manpower to occasional technological innovations. The latest phenomenon, the so-called micro-electronic revolution, may not be an exception, either. The truth is that technological progress has been taking place continually. Ideally, therefore, accumulated data over a reasonably long period of time should be examined. Nevertheless, the year 1977 was four years after the first oil shock of 1973 and one year before the second oil shock of 1978. 1977 therefore seems a reasonably good year to indicate how Japanese enterprises dealt with the problem of producing more value-added products with less energy and resources, including labor.

The data were taken from the 1977 Survey on Employment Management published by Statistics and Information Department, Minister's Secretariat, Ministry of Labor. This is the only national data available (7,000 enterprises were systematically sampled out of those with more than 30 employees) which contain information about firms' recruitment policies for regular workers, firms' ideas on labor management, policies and practices of intrafirm transfer, and retraining methods. In addition to its uniqueness in kind, the above data set are coded by industry and firm size, and are suitable for the type of analysis attempted in this paper.

Hypotheses and Findings

A large-size enterprise tends to have a large stock of
capital, a larger number of employees, and a wider range
of production activities. It has generally been established many years ago, and has a wealth of skilled
workers. It also tends to have a well-structured training
program for the newly hired and for the incumbents.

It is therefore expected that (1) the incidence of
intrafirm transfers is more frequent in a larger enterprise; (2) Given a wealth of skilled workers and training
facilities, retraining takes place more easily in a
larger enterprise; (3) With a greater scope of production
activities and processes, a larger enterprise has more
room for transfers to a different job and thus incurs a
greater necessity of retraining the transferred.

In order to put these hypotheses to an indirect test, a
series of Charts 7 through 18 was constructed based on
the survey data.

Chart 11 and 12 do not refute Hypothesis 1. The percentage of enterprises engaged in intrafirm transfers
generally increases as the size of the firm gets larger,
going from 30-99 employees to 5,000 and more employees.
The relationship between the incidence of intrafirm
transfers and enterprise size is monotonically positive
with respect to a transfer to a different job. This
relation holds both for the unskilled and the skilled
workers. An unskilled worker is definded in this survey
as a worker who engages in simple manual labor of a
miscellaneous type. A skilled worker is definded as a
worker who engages in a job which requires a high level
of skill, decision-making, and responsibility, and which
requires therefore both oft-the-job-training Off-JT and
On-the-job-training OJT after the hiring (this category
includes a semi-skilled worker since he is regarded as on
the way to becoming skilled). A similarly positive

Chart 7

Ratio of firms engaged in retraining of the un-skilled for the same job (1977)

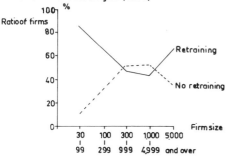

Chart 8

Ratio of firms engaged in retraining of the un-skilled for another job (1977)

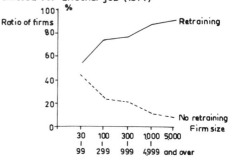

Chart 9

Ratio of firms engaged in retraining of the skilled for the same job (1977)

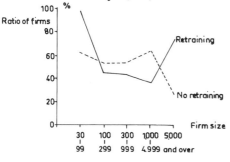

Chart 10

Ratio of firms engaged in retraining of the skilled for another job (1977)

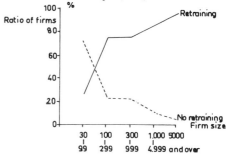

Chart 11

Ratio of firms by way of transfer of the unskilled (1977)

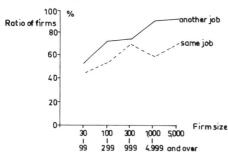

Chart 12

Ratio of firms by way of transfer of the skilled (1977)

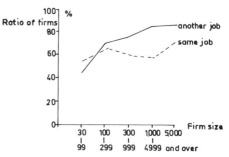

Source: Survey on Employment Management, Ministry of Labor, 1977.

Design: Toda
Graphicdesign: IFEP Freiburg i. Br. Kö 87.2

Chart 13

Ratio of firms engaged in retraining of the unskilled for the same job in manufacturing (1977)

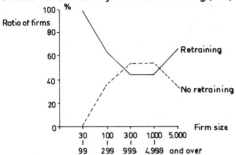

Chart 14

Ratio of firms engaged in retraining of the unskilled for another job in manufacturing (1977)

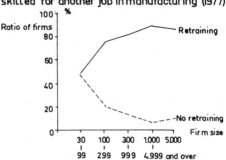

Chart 15

Ratio of firms engaged in retraining of the
skilled for the same job in manufacturing(1977)

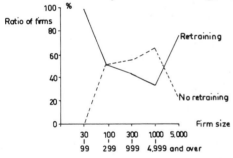

Chart 16

Ratio of firms engaged in retraining of the
skilled for another job in manufacturing (1977)

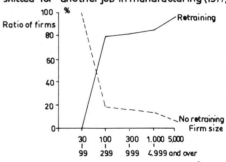

Chart 17

Ratio of firms by way of transfer of the
unskilled in manufacturing (1977)

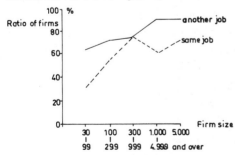

Chart 18

Ratio of firms by way of transfer of the
skilled in manufacturing (1977)

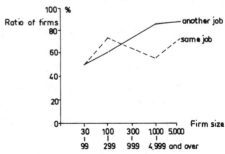

Source : Survey on Employment Management, Ministry of Labor, 1977.

Design: Toda

Graphicdesign: IFEP Freiburg i. Br. Kö 87.2

relation holds for a transfer within the enterprise, although the incidence rate of the-same-job transfer is universally lower than the other job transfer, except that the same job transfer exceeds the other in the catecory of smallest sized firms (30-99 employees) in the case of skilled workers (Chart 12).

For the-same-job transfer, irrespective of the level of skill, the relation gets reversed from the 300-999 size to the 1,000-4,999 size. We simply note here the anomaly of the 1,000-4,999 category without attempting any explanation for this phenomenon.

These patterns, singled out for manufacturing alone (Charts 17 and 18), resembled greatly those of industry as a whole, except that there the anomalous category of 1,000-4,999 employees is even more accentuated. This size of enterprise may mark some turning point for organizational efficiency, economies of scale, capital-output ratio, and technology transfer within the organization. Other than this rather ad hoc enumeration, we have no explanation for this phenomenon at this point.

We now turn to a test of Hypothesis 2. It was hypothesized above that due to a wealth of skilled workers and training facilities, retraining takes place more easily in a larger enterprise. A contrary result was obtained. While retraining of the unskilled for the other job takes place more often as firm size grows (Charts 8 and 14), the pattern of retraining of the unskilled for the same job becomes bi-modal, high in the two extreme sizes of 30-99 and 5,000 and more employees (Charts 7 and 13). There were no noticeable differences in pattern between total industry and manufacturing. The question to be answered is why such a great percentage of small firms provide unskilled workers who are transferred to the same type of job with vocational training even more frequently than in very large firms. Training pattern of the skilled repeated the above results (Charts 9 and 15). In the-same-job transfer a large percentage of very small firms and of very large firms train their transferred employees (irrespective of skill level), while the incidence of training in firms of medium size is low.

For the skilled, the anomalous category of firms with 1,000-4,999 employees has a much lower probability of retraining, along with a lower probability in the 100-299 employee category, as compared with the case for the unskilled. It should be noted that in this Survey the numbers of transfers do not include any routine personnel moves, but count only the transfers necessitated by internal adjustment of the excess work force.

As to Hypothesis 3, which is simply a paraphrase of Hypotheses 1 and 2, the findings represented by the series of Charts 7 through 18 are not inconsistent with the hypothesis, although a more direct test is not possible without more detailed data.

In sum, the larger the size of an enterprise, the more likely the enterprise will engage in intrafirm transfer of employees. If the worker is unskilled and works in a very large enterprise, he almost certainly will be given an opportunity for retraining if he has been transferred to a different job. However, if the worker was sent to a new job of the same type, he is less likely to be retrained unless he works either at a very small or very large firm. If the worker is skilled, he will have a far less chance of getting retrained either in the 100-299 or 1,000-4,999 employees size enterprise. Why two such opposite sizes of firms encourage retraining, while firms of the in-between size do not, and why the 100-299 and the 1,000-4,999 employees sizes of firms do not carry out retraining of the skilled, are two important yet unanswered questions.

II 5   The Effect of Technological Change and Work
         Environment on the Rate of Transfer: Regression
         Analysis based on a 1982 Survey on Technological
         Innovation and Labor

In order to tackle the two unresolved puzzles mentioned
in the previous subsection (II 4), we will examine in
this section the characteristics of intrafirm transfer
under microelectronic innovation. For this inquiry,
requirements for data are severe. The following data must
be available for a very recent year in the microelectronic (ME) revolution: rate of intrafirm transfer in
manufacturing, the extent of use of microelectronics in
each industry, changes in skill requirements in the
production line after the introduction of ME equipment,
changes in factory employment and in the amount of new
hiring after that introduction.

The Ministry of Labor has just released part of such data
and we took advantage of it here. It is called the Survey
on Technological Innovation and Labor.[7] It was conducted
in November of 1982, when there already existed several
surveys done by a government agency, a labor union, and a
private organization. But the scope of the sample and the
questions asked in these studies were very limited, and a
comprehensive survey was called for. In response to this
demand, the Ministry conducted the first national survey
of approximately 10,000 private establishments with more
than 100 regular production workers in the manufacturing
sector.

This survey, however, did not inquire into the rate of
intrafirm transfer, and this information from the 1982
Survey on Employment Trend was supplemented in our
empirical analysis here. The definitions and sources of
data used are listed in Table 1.

TABLE 1   Definitions of Variables, Mean Values, and Source

Variable	Definition	Mean Value	Source
TRANS	the percentage ratio of the trans-ferred within the same enterprise to the total number of regular em-ployees on the First of January	3.39	1982 Survey on Employment Trend, Ministry of Labor
INTRO	the percentage ratio of establish-ments using equipment with IC in an industry	56.64	1982 Survey on Technological Inno-vation and Labor, Ministry of Labor
HISTRY	the percentage ratio of establish-ments which has introduced equip-ments with IC before 1974	27.71	1982 Survey on Technological Innovation and Labor, Ministry of Labor
REASON	The percentage ratio of establish-ments whose main aim of intro-duction was to promote labor-saving (multiple-answers question)	61.92	1982 Survey on Technological Innovation and Labor, Ministry of Labor
SKILL	the percentage ratio of the pro-duction processes in which skill requirement has changed with intro-duction of equipment with IC for all the processes using them	64.93	1982 Survey on Technological Inno-vation and Labor, Ministry of Labor
REDUC	the percentage ratio of the estab-lishment which decreased the number of workers for all the establish-ments using equipment with IC in an industry	30.05	1982 Survey on Technological Inno-vation and Labor, Ministry of Labor
HIRES	the percentage ratio of the estab-lishments which showed a great change in the number of newly hired employees	9.69	1982 Survey on Technological Inno-vation and Labor, Ministry of Labor

Determinants of the Rate of Intrafirm Transfer

As was clear from our discussion of the natur of ME
innovation (Section II 3), introduction of ME equipment
brings about a reshuffling of the work force in the
production line. One can therefore expect that the
greater the ratio of establishments using equipment with
integrated circuits (IC), the higher will be the rate of
intrafirm transfer in that industry, which is defined as
the ratio of the transferred to the total number of
regular employees in that industry.

The earlier microelectronics were introduced into a
factory, the deeper its effects were on the size and
composition of the work force at the site. Thus, a
greater number of transfers may be taking place at those
establishments in which the microelectronic revolution
has been well under way.

If a main motive for introducing ME into an enterprise is
to save labor, it is naturally to be expected that its
introduction will cause a decrease in labor, and under
the assumption of layoff-resistant practices, the incidence of intrafirm transfer will increase.

Changes in job content inevitably occur. Polarization of
tasks into simple manual work and highly technical and
skill-specific work tends to cause frequent reshuffling
of workers at the production line. That is, as skill
requirements in the production process change, transfers
are likely to occur.

The incidence of transfer is of course influenced by the
personnel policies of an enterprise. First, if a
reduction of the work force has already taken place at an
establishment, the enterprise simply does not have
persons to move at that establishment, and transfer is
less likely to happen. Secondly, they will have a subtle
impact upon the rate of transfer whether an enterprise

increases or decreases its new hiring. Directions of its impact, however, cannot be asserted a priori, and it is genuinely an empirical question.

Empirical Results

The results of the estimation are presented in Table 2. The results indicate that an enterprise which introduced microelectronic equipment before 1974 and also uses it currently tends to have a higher rate of intrafirm transfer (out and into). Other factors such as labor-saving policy, employment reduction, and hiring policy do not appear to be statistically significant to explain the behavior of an enterprise's transfer policy.

Although it will not be listed here due to space limitation, simple correlation between variables provides us with information which cannot be omitted. Some of the significant relations are the following: An industry which makes good use of microelectronic equipment at the current time is likely to be one that started using it more than 8 years ago (simple correlation was .743). Industry with a larger share of establishments using microelectronics is likely to experience changing skill requirements at production line (simple correlation between INTRO and SKILL was .818). Also, an industry with a longer history of microelectronic production tends to observe the changes in skill requirement (simple correlation between HISTRY and SKILL was .607).

As to the measurement of the incidence of intrafirm transfers, two different proxies were used. TRANS(ALL) measure both those transferred out of and into the same enterprise, whereas TRANS(OUT) includes only those transferred out.

The regression results in Table 2 show that whether an enterprise (an industry) has introduced microelectronics,

TABLE 2 Regression Results: Determinants of Intrafirm Transfer
(t-statistics in parentheses)

Dependent Variable	cons.	Independent Variables						$\bar{R}^2$	N
		INTRO	HISTRY	REASON	SKILL	REDUC	HIRES		
TRANS(ALL)	4.001	.121***	.095**	-.020	-.171***	.086	.041	.815	18
		(3.37)	(2.82)	(.51)	(3.32)	(1.94)	(.65)		
TRANS(OUT)	1.480	.076***	.040	-.012	-.089**	.053	-.012	.788	18
		(3.47)	(1.99)	(.51)	(2.88)	(1.98)	(.31)		

Note: TRANS(ALL) = the percentage ratio of the sum of the transferred (transfer out and transfer into) within the same enterprise to the total number of regular employees in an industry on the First of January.

TRANS(OUT) = the percentage ratio of the tranferred out within the same enterprise to the total number of regular employees in an industry on the First of January.

18 of the two-digit manufacturing industries are:
food and tabacco; textile mill products; apparel and other finished products made from fabrics and similar materials; lumber and wood products; furniture and fixtures; pulp paper and paper worked products; publishing, printing and allied industries; chemical, petroleum, coal products; rubber and leather; ceramic, stone and clay products; iron and steel; non-ferrous metals and products; fabricated metal products; machinery; electrical machinery; transportation equipment; precision machinery; weapon industry and other manufacturing

** Significant at the 1 percent level, one-tail test.
*** Significant at the 0.5 percent level, one-tail test.

and how long it has been carrying out its production using IC-equipment are the two major factors that explain the rate of intrafirm transfer.

Although basically similar results were obtained for the TRANS(OUT) estimation, two subtleties are noted here. The INTRO variable was more statistically significant in the TRANS(OUT) equation and the SKILL variable also showed a significance in it. It may follow that (1) the effect of introduction of MEs works more strongly on the trans-ferred out, thereby reducing employment unless reduction is more than offset by an influx of newly hired workers and the transferred into, and that (2) greater changes in skill requirement tend to decrease the rate of transfer. This second finding may be interpreted such, that a new mode of production using microelectronics, has to utilize the skill-specificity of skilled production worker, in spite of the new production method, and therefore will retain them rather than eliminating them. This is not inconsistent with the findings of some of the previous studies.

Despite our expectations, all other independent variables (REASON; REDUC and HIRES) could not determine any statistical strength in either of the two specifications above. It is necessary to explore these aspects as new and more detailed statistical information comes along in the near future. Also, our interpretation of the empirical results presented here may be too hasty in view of the fact that an enterprise shifts its work force for many different reasons. It will transfer its workers internally due to (1) routine personnel policy, (2) labor saving plan, (3) temporary help necessitated by an expansion of production and business, (4) reduction in work force due to a shrinking of production and business, (5) allotment policy for the middle-aged and the old employees, and (6) personal request from an employee. The data used here do not distinguish among these reasons and tend to blur the effect of ME introduction on the internal allocation of labor.

III   A Reconsideration of the Retraining of the Trans-
ferred Employees

III 1   Evidence from Other Studies

Despite some statistical ambiguity the empirical analysis in the previous section indicates a strong relation between the introduction of microelectronics and the incidence of intrafirm transfer. The difficulty here is to ascertain the direction of the causality. Whether the introduction of ME causes an increase in transfers will remain an unresolved empirical question until a detailed national survey has been conducted. It may be simply that a large enterprise tends to have a greater frequency of internal transfer, and that a large enterprise has a greater cash flow which enables it to install expensive equipment involving IC. If this is the case, an observed positive relation between TRANS(ALL) and INTRO turns out to be spurious.

For the time being, nevertheless, it seems safe to say something about the effect of ME on the internal allocation of labor with a special emphasis on the retraining policies of enterprises, if our focus of attention is limited to the manufacturing sector which is generally thought to be the mother industry of computers.

We now return to another consideration of the retraining policies of enterprises for their transferred employees. Among all the studies, small and large, conducted to date, only a few have included questions concerning retraining under microelectronic innovation. This section will utilize evidence taken from those studies in order to reconsider our two unresolved puzzles: (1) why do two opposite sizes of firms encourage retraining while firms of the in-between size do not, irrespective of whether the workers involved are skilled or unskilled, and (2)

why do the 100-299 and the 1,0004,999 employee sizes of
firms not carry out retraining, specifically, of the
skilled workers?

1982 Survey on the Effective Use of Manpower with a
Special Reference to Technological Innovation and Utilization of "Graypower"

This survey was conducted by a study group on enterprise
training with the assistance of the Ministry of Labor in
March, 1982. It covered approximately 4,400 establishments in manufacturing and approximately 15,000 skilled
workers employed there. The survey was conducted in the
form of a questionnaire, but 30 establishments were
actually interviewed by members of the study group.

Table 3 shows the choices of instruction methods for ME
operators according to establishment size, and reveals
that large enterprises marshal significantly more
resources for manpower development under technological
innovation than smaller firms do.

The patterns of retraining the transferred employees, as
presented in (Table 4) are similar, regardless of
enterprise size. The percentage ratio of establishments
in each mode of training is greater for a larger
enterprise. (Note that we are using the words "establishment" and "enterprise" interchangeably, although they
should be strictly distinguished in a strict sense).

TABLE 3   Instruction Methods for ME Operators
(Ratio of establishments; multiple answers)

Instruction Method	Total	Size of Firm 30-99	100-999	over 1000 Employees
a. training by seller	65.3	65.1	67.0	62.3
b. commercial training	23.1	17.6	27.5	32.2
c. self training	46.6	37.1	47.6	80.1
d. correspondence	6.1	1.8	7.8	17.6
e. OJT	66.0	57.3	71.2	83.9
f. Nothing	3.2	4.9	2.0	0.0

Note: Only those establishments using IC-equipment were questioned.
Source: Report on the 1982 Survey on the Effective Use of Manpower, p.40

TABLE 4   Retraining the Transferred Middle-aged and older Workers
(Ratio of Establishments; multiple answers)

Retraining Procedure	Total	Size of Firm 30-99	100-999	over 1000
a. off the job group training (Off-JT) prior to transfer (Off-JT) after transfer	25.5	22.1	26.0	41.2
b. on the job training (OJT) after transfer	26.4	21.5	28.1	43.5
c.	75.8	69.9	83.2	83.6
d. Transfer to jobs that do not require re-training	18.3	22.3	15.4	8.5

Note: Only those establishments which indicated a possiblility of intrafirm transfer for the middle- and old-aged worker were questioned.
Source: Report on the 1982 Survey on the Effective Use of Manpower, p.79

Chart 19

Composition of Skilled Workers by Educational Level

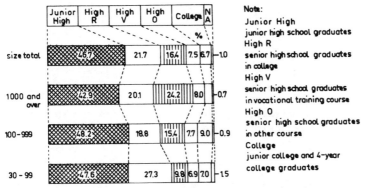

Note:
Junior High
junior high school graduates
High R
senior high school graduates
in college
High V
senior high school graduates
in vocational training course
High O
senior high school graduates
in other course
College
junior college and 4-year
college graduates

Source: Report on 1982 Survey on Effective Use of Manpower, p. 99

Chart 19 above reveals a partial answer to our puzzle. It was found that firms, regardless of size, prefer to hire for a vocational training course senior high school graduates well over their counterparts in college preparatory courses (The chart is not shown here due to space limitation). Firms like them because they have received a technical education, and are less resistant to the idea of being a production worker. They also think that senior high school graduates are generally more able than junior high school graduates. According to Chart 19, which shows the composition of skilled production workers by establishment size and by attained level of education, the 100-999 employee size category has the largest share of college graduates and junior high school graduates, and the smallest share of senior high school graduates in college preparatory courses among the three different size categories of establishments. The 100-999 employee-size establishments do not carry out extensive training for their skilled work force if they think that (1) college graduates, the ablest group, do not require training, (2) junior high graduates, the least able group, are not very trainable, and that (3) senior high graduates with no vocational training need training.

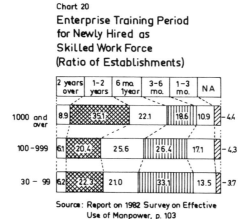

Chart 20

Enterprise Training Period for Newly Hired as Skilled Work Force (Ratio of Establishments)

Source: Report on 1982 Survey on Effective Use of Manpower, p. 103

Another clue to the puzzle is found in the lengths of the training periods which the enterprises conduct in order to train the newly hired to become skilled laborers. The 100-999 employee-size establishments have the smallest shares in the longer training periods (1 to 2 years and more than two years) and the largest share in the shorter training periods (1 to 3 months and 6 months to 1 year) among the three different size categories of establishments (Chart 20).

Interestingly enough, skilled workers at the establishments of 100-999 employees seek the most OJT, outside Off-JT with support of an enterprise, and training through transfer or temporary help among the three different size categories of establishments (Table 5).

In sum, establishments in the 100-999 employee category have a larger percentage of junior high school graduates and college graduates, and therefore a weaker incentive to retrain their skilled workers than the smallest and the largest categories of firms do. Contrary to these retraining policies of the enterprises, the skilled workers employed at them strongly with to be given more extensive opportunities for various types of training. And, as was seen, resources for training or manpower development are more scarce at smaller establishments. Thus, public or private support for retraining in the medium-sized establishments can be an effective manpower policy in the sense that it will at least give its skilled work force a higher morale and an incentive to work more efficiently under technological innovation.

The 1981 Survey on Internal Labor Utilization

The Institute for Employment and Occupational Research surveyed 1,432 member and non-member firms of stock exchanges in December, 1981. The survey inquired as to whether an employer feels he has an excess number of employees in a certain type of job. Part of the responses are tabulated in Table 6.

Another clue to our puzzle was obtained. The degrees of excess employment vary according to type of job and firm size, contrary to the general notion that only the largest-sized firms tend to have more employees than they need. As revealed by Table 6, the medium-sized firms, specifically the groups 300-999 and 1,000-2,999, do tend to employ an excessive work force in skilled jobs and R & D design jobs categories. For male employees as a whole, the 1,000-2,999 size category is the foremost excessive employer.

Although it does not necessarily follow that training is not needed in order to attain an ample size of the work force, it can be said at least that an employer has more room for allotting a better qualified to the job, thereby reducing the necessity of training. Thus, the employment

TABLE 5   Training Methods Preferred by Skilled Workers
(%; multiple answers)

Training Method Preferred	Size of Firm		
	30-99	100-999	1,000 and over
a. Self training by firm	37.6	45.0	56.4
b. OJT	30.8	32.8	31.6
c. Voluntary study group	15.0	13.8	13.6
d. Training through help and transfer	2.9	4.9	2.8
e. Outside Off-JT with support of the firm	29.9	32.2	28.6
f. Outside Off-JT with self support	18.4	17.5	13.9
g. Correspondence course	11.5	12.1	19.3

Source: Report on the 1982 Survey on the Effective Use of Manpower, p. 207

TABLE 6 Ratio of Firms which Responded as Having an Excess Work Force

Job Category		Size of Firm				
	5-29	30-99	100-299	300-999	1000-2999	3000 over
male employees	2.2	7.2	9.6	11.5	15.8***	10.9
female employees	5.0	5.2	7.6	7.2	4.8	7.8
a. R & D design	0.0	1.2	1.9	4.7**	2.4	3.3
b. male sales	0.0	1.4	4.1	2.7	2.6	2.2
c. female sales	0.0	2.3	2.1	2.2	3.3	1.4
d. skilled (male)	0.0	4.1	8.4	9.6	14.4**	9.9
e. transportation	3.7	4.4	5.0	3.5	9.1	7.1
f. service	0.0	4.5	4.7	0.0	4.3	2.7
g. male clerk	1.4	3.8	7.3	11.7*	13.9**	13.2
h. female clerk	2.7	4.0	6.5	8.3	8.0	6.6

Note: *** Significant at the 1 percent level, critical ratio test.
 ** Significant at the 5 percent level, critical ratio test.
  * Significant at the 10 percent level, critical ratio test.

Source: Report on the 1981 Survey on Internal Labor Utilization, p.9

structures and job distribution among industries and among different sizes of enterprises appear to be the major factors that should not be neglected in the analysis of technological change and training in enter- prises.

Chart 21
Ratio of Firms Which Rotate Workers Regularly or Occasionally by Firm Size

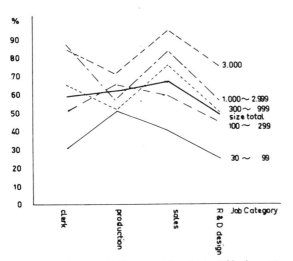

Source: Report on 1981 Survey on Internal Labor Utilization, p. 138

An approach based on human capital theory will also resolve part of our puzzle. According to this approach, people can be trained mainly in two ways: schooling and OJT. In the schooling method, irrespective of the location of the schooling (at a school or at a firm), workers are removed from the production line and costs are far from negligible when measured in terms of lost man-hours and production. When training has to be con- tinued over a long period of time, it is cheaper to train workers on the job. Professor Koike, for example, advocates on OJT retraining method in order to cope with

microelectronic revolution at a factory from a cost-bene-
fit viewpoint.[8] In any case, the substitutability
between schooling and OJT is clear. And, as was seen in
the above, smaller firms have less resources for various
types of training. A firm may therefore opt for the
cheapest kind - OJT. This seems to be what actually
happened. The firms in the 100-299 employee- size
category rotated their production workers regularly or
occasionally much more than firms in the other three
(1,000-2,999, 300-999, and 30-99) categories, as shown in
Chart 21. If in reference to 'retraining' they meant
Off-JT, then the less frequent incidence of 'retraining'
at the firms of the 100-299 employee-size can be explained by this substitutability hypothesis, and part of
our puzzle is resolved.

Koike's Report on The Impact of Microelectronics on
Employment (1982)

Professor Koike of Kyoto University headed an Osaka
Prefectural study group which conducted questionnaire
surveys on 3,982 establishments and interviews with 18
establishments in October, 1982. One of his results
illuminates what we have just said in the previous
subsection of III 1.

If an enterprise rotates a worker regularly or occasionally, he is likely to pick up skill experience with
related but different types of jobs in the production
lines. This allround and firm-specific skill experience
must fit a new skill requirement under technological
changes at the factory. If the 100-499 employee-size firm
is more likely to rotate its workers than the other sizes
of firms, it will be expected that it attains programmers
or system engineers from the currently employed machine
operators rather than the other groups.

144

This is indeed what was taking place. Chart 22 and 23 testify that the 100-499 employee category ranks top among the firms which attain their programmers or system engineers by training through ME operators. This finding strengthens our inference that a mediumsize firm tends to rotate its employees since it is a cost-effective way of training at a resource-hungry establishment.

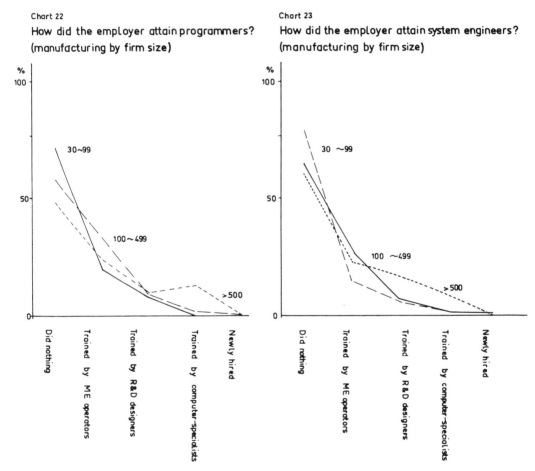

Chart 22

How did the employer attain programmers?
(manufacturing by firm size)

Chart 23

How did the employer attain system engineers?
(manufacturing by firm size)

Source: Koike's Report on the Impact of Microelectronics on Employment, pp. 60-61

IV   Summary and Conclusion

Induced changes in employment and job content in the microelectronic environment have been the focus of attention in numerous public and private surveys conducted since 1981.

New forms of automation, represented by numerical control and machining center machine tools and robots, make an existing skill obsolete and demand a flexible, highly intelligent, and technical production worker with problem-solving ability.

How to make labor fit into this new mode of production is of great concern not only for an individual firm but also for a national economy and industrial relations. Even if firms can fire freely an excess of obsolete and unfit laborers, attainment of the necessary labor is a challenge to a nation's educational system and industrial policy. A constraint that the life-long employment practice in Japan puts on individual firms simply doubles this challenge. Viewed in this light, an inquiry into the relation between technological change and human resources development through vocational training and manpower deployment is essential, and this paper attempts a first small stept in this direction.

First, it was found that intrafirm transfer has been a major internal adjustment instrument. It was, however, cautioned that a larger firm tends to reshuffle its work force because of a wider scope of production activities and a larger number of positions. It is almost impossible to delineate the increased or decreased incidence of internal transfer due to the introduction of equipment using integrated circuits until a more detailed national sample is gathered in the near future.

Nevertheless, as is clear from the theory of internal labor markets and the theory of human capital, that it is quite rational for an employer to retain enterprise-specificaly skilled workers, to transfer them to a related job, to revitalize their accumulated experience through Off-JT and OJT, to raise productivity and to generate more value-added products in the market. While this is common in any firm or industry (manufacturing is currently most important), it is expected that the way this common objective is reached will differ, because the costs and benefits associated differ among firms of various sizes and amounts of capital formation.

What was found was not a dichotomy between large and small sized firms, but a trichotomy between large, medium, and small sizes. The medium-sized category of firms behave quite uniquely, while the two extreme sizes form a rather similar pattern as to retraining policies of the skilled an the unskilled workers. Large (5,000 and over employees) and small (30-99 employees) firms encourage retraining, while the 100-299 and the 1,000-4,999 employee sizes of firms do not carry out retraining of the skilled.

In order to resolve this apparent puzzle, surveyed data from various sources were examined. Our findings are as follows.

(1) Quality of the labor force: It was found that firms, regardless of size, much prefer to hire for skilled work senior high school graduates in their vocational training courses, over the counterparts in college preparatory courses. Firms like them because they have received a technical education, and are less resistant to the idea of being a production worker. They also think that senior high school graduates are generally abler than junior high school graduates. The 100-999 employee-size category has the largest share of college graduates and junior high school graduates, and the smallest share of senior high

school graduates in college preparatory course among
the three different size categories (30-99 and 1,000
and over) of establishments. The 100-999 employee-
size establishments do not carry out an extensive
training of their skilled work force if they think
that college graduates, the ablest group, do not
require training, that junior high graduates, the
least able group, are not very trainable, and that
senior high graduates, with no previous vocational
training need training.

(2) Training Period: Among the 100-999 employee- size
establishments the three different size categories of
establishments have the smallest share in the longer
training periods (1 to 2 years and more than 2 years)
and the largest share in the shorter training periods
(1 to 3 months and 6 months to 1 year).

(3) Employee opinion: Skilled workers at the establishments of 100-999 employees seek the most OJT, the
most outside Off-JT with support of an enterprise,
and the most training through transfer or temporary
help among the three different size categories of
establishments.

(4) Employment structure and job distribution: The
degrees of excess employment vary according to the
type of job and firm size, contrary to a general
notion that only the largest sized firms tend to have
more employees than they need. The medium sized
firms, specifically those in the 300-999 and 1,000-
2,999 groups, do tend to employ an excessive work
force in skilled jobs and R & D design job categories. For male employees as a whole, the 1,000-2,999
size category is the foremost excessive employer.
Although it does not necessarily follow that training
is not needed for an amply sized work force, the
least one can say is that an employer has more room
for alloting a better qualified person to a job,

thereby reducing the necessity of training. Thus, the employment structures and job distribution among industries and among different sizes of enterprises appear to be the major factors that should not be neglected in the analysis of technological change and training by enterprises.

(5) Substitution effect (substitutability between schooling and OJT): People can be trained mainly in two ways: schooling and OJT. In the schooling method irrespective of the location of the schooling (at a school or at a firm), workers are separated from the production line and costs are far from negligible when measured in terms of lost man-hours and production. When training has to be continued over a long period of time, it is cheaper to train workers on the job. Smaller firms have less resources for various types of training. A firm may therefore opt for the cheapest kind: OJT. The firms in the 100-299 employee-size category rotated, their workers regularly or occasionally much more so than firms in the other three (1,000-2,999, 300-999, and 30-99) categories.

(6) Career formation through job rotation: If an enterprise rotates a worker regularly or occasionally, he is likely to pick up skill experience with related but different types of jobs at production lines. This all-round and firm-specific skill experience must fit new skill requirements due to technological changes at the factory. The 100-499 employee category ranks top among the firms which attained programmers or system engineers trained by ME operators. A medium-sized firm tends to rotate its employees since it is a cost-effective way of training at a resource-poor establishment.

Resources for training or manpower development are more scarce at smaller establishments. Thus, public or private support for retraining at medium-sized establishments can be an effective manpower policy in the sense that it will, at the least, give its skilled work force a higher morale and an incentive to work more efficiently under technological innovation.

Schooling and OJT can be complementary to each other in certain aspects of the training process. An optimal mix of the two can be determined by recruiting and by the financial resource allocation policy of an enterprise.

NOTES

1. See Taira (11) for an illuminating account of the Japanese economic scene after the first oil shock of 1973.

2. See Muramatsu (9)

3. See, for example, Ministry of Labor (5)

4. See Doeringer and Piore (1)

5. See, for example, Koike (4).

6. An account followed was basically taken from Koike (4).

7. For a concise summary of the main results of this survey, see Institute for Personnel Administration (3).

8. Koike (4), p. 19.

REFERENCES

DOERINGER, P.B. and PIORE, M.J.: Internal Labor Markets and Manpower Analysis. Lexington, Mass.: D.C. Heath, 1971.

INSTITUTE FOR FMPLOYMENT AND OCCUPATIONAL RESEARCH: 1981 Survey on Internal Labor Utilization.

INSTITUTE FOR PERSONNEL ADMINISTRATION: Personnel Administration Monthly, October, 1983, pp. 3-29.

KOIKE, KAZUO: Report on The Impact of Microelectronics on Employment. Dept. of Labor, Osaka Prefecture, 1982.

MINISTRY OF LABOR: Survey on Technological Innovation and Labor (Gijutsu Kakushin to Rodo ni Kansuru Chosa), 1982.

MINISTRY OF LABOR: Report on 1982 Survey on Effective Use of Manpower, 1982.

MINISTRY OF LABOR: 1977 Survey on Employment Management. (Koyo Kanri Chosa).

MINISTRY OF LABOR: 1982 Survey on Employment Trend. (Koyo Doko Chosa).

MURAMATSU, K.: Analysis of Japanese Labor Market, 1981.

OSAKA PRODUCTIVITY CENTER ed.: Electromechanics Revolution and Industrial Policy, 1983.

TAIRA, K.: "Industrial Policy and Employment in Japan", Current Histry, Nov. 1983, pp. 362-365.

Innovative Investment and Taxation in the Federal Republic of Germany

Hans-Hermann Francke

A The Problem

Undoubtedly one of the important causes of the present unemployment in the FRG is the lack of investment, which has become apparent in the last ten years. Of course, there may be many different reasons for this deficiency, but one of them, namely the tax policy, plays a prominent role in the current discussion of this problem. In particular the opinion of the German Council of Economic Advisers (Sachverständigenrat zur Begutachtung der gesamtwirtschaftlichen Entwicklung) repeated the thesis that the German system of taxation is not only disadvantageous for the investment of productive capital, but it also discriminates against innovations.

Following the Council - and many other economists agree with this thesis - there are two main reasons for the negative impact of the taxation system on innovative investment:

1. The possibilities for offsetting losses incurred through risky investments are insufficient in the German tax system, so that the tendency to undertake innovative investment is lessened.

2. The financing of innovative investment is even more difficult, because the formation and supply of risk-bearing capital is discriminated against by taxation.

So, the Council has made several proposals to change the system of taxation in order to promote innovative investment. The purpose of this paper is to explain the dominant points of the critique and to discuss some of the proposals for a change in tax policy.

B Theoretical Impact of Taxation on Risk-Taking

I Risk of Innovative Investment

Of course, every investor undertakes a risk, because his investment is based on uncertain expectations of probable returns in the future. There is no way to escape this problem; but it is possible to rationalize it by comparing the probable gains and losses of an investment. The usual method of making such a comparison is to calculate the mathematical expectations of the probable gains and losses as well as the measures of dispersion of the probable rates of return. The latter may serve as a proxy for the expected risk of the investment. The decision to invest or not to invest then depends on the mathematical expectation of the rates of return and the risk proxy, which may be the range of the expected gains and losses or the standard deviation or another suitable measure of dispersion. The investor's propensitiy to bear the risk of an investment may then be characterized by the magnitude of the accepted risk at given levels of expected net rates of return. If the investor likes risk-taking (because increasing risks are usually connected with increasing returns), he will - at given levels of expected return - accept a higher risk than another investor, who shows risk aversion.

The thesis that innovative investment is usually more risky than traditional investment does not seem to be always plausible. But we will take it as given insofar as in the case of innovative investment, it is impossible to calculate probable gains and losses on the basis of the experiences of the past. So the expectations of the probable net rates of return should take into consideration a relatively high dispersion among them.

II Taxation and Investment Risk

Following the portfolio-selection theory, the theory of taxation developed many models to analyze the influence of taxation on risky investment. But, in general, the results of these models were ambiguous. They were ambiguous, because they revealed that there are several possibilities: taxation can have either an increasing, decreasing, or neutral effect on risky investment, when a general tax on income or net-returns is imposed. These ambiguous results are due to the effect of taxation on the risk, which in many cases will be reduced by the tax.

This - at first glance surprising - result depends on the fact, that, if a tax offset for losses is permitted, the taxes reduce not only the returns, but also partially lower the risk, because the dispersion of the probable gains and losses of the investment will be reduced. So the government becomes the partner of the investor and perhaps may increase the overall tendency to take risks. Whether the amount of investment will increase is not a priori clear. The investor has to compare the negative effect of the reduced expected net return and the positive effect of the reduced risk. In the case of very risky investments, the latter effect may be dominant, but this is not certain.

The role of depreciation in the investment formation process is in a similar sense ambiguous. Depreciation reduces the effective rate of taxation by postponing the date of the tax liability. For a single investment this means a gain in the form of interest earnings and liquidity in spite of the fact that the total amount of taxes to be paid over the whole period of earnings will not be reduced. For a revolving and growing investment, the investor is able to postpone the tax payment indefinitely. So, the effect of speeding up depreciation on the expected net return of the investment is undoutedly positive. But whether risky investments are increased by easier depreciation regulations is not clear. If depreciation is possible for investment with both high and low risk, then the tax gain for the low-risk investment is relatively higher. As a result some investors may prefer investments with lower risk.

Therefore one has to be sceptical towards the popular thesis that a tax reduction will always stimulate innovative investment. Nevertheless, in spite of the ambiguous results of these basic theoretical considerations we have achieved insight into two crucial aspects of the problem: The first is the importance of a tax offset for losses. An increase in the possibilities to offset losses will decrease the risk for the investor. The second crucial point is that the overall effects of general taxes on investment are not clear. So, in order to stimulate innovative investment it may be more useful to discriminate against investments with lower risk through taxation.

C Characteristics of the German System of Taxation

I General Systematic Aspects

From the general systematic viewpoint the popular criticism against the investment effects of the existing system of taxation are twofold: on the one hand it has been criticized that there are some taxes which must be paid independently of earnings, such as the tax on working capital (Gewerbekapitalsteuer) and the wealth-tax. On the other hand, there is the - often repeated - proposal to reduce the relative share of direct taxes, especially personal and corporate income tax, in favor of the indirect taxes, especially the German value-added sales tax and other special sales taxes.

The argument behind the first point of criticism is quite clear and convincing. A tax which has to be paid on wealth, regardless of whether there are earnings or not, has a negative impact on the formation of capital goods. The importance of this negative impact will rise when the investment becomes riskier. For if there are losses, the tax has to be paid from the existing stock of wealth, so that the capital-owner loses part of his wealth. Therefore the proposal to abolish the tax on working capital and perhaps change the system of taxing wealth deserves support. Nevertheless, the problem should not be exaggerated, because the share of these taxes is relatively small (less than 5 % of the whole tax revenues).

The second point of criticism seems to be much more complicated and, as I believe, the popular view contains some serious shortcomings. Proponents of the relative increase in sales taxes hold the thesis that sales taxes, and especially the German value-added tax, have a positive effect on the growth rate to the extent that they do not affect investment and tax only the consumer. Therefore the system of taxation should be changed in such a way that the relative role of income taxes decreases.

In my opinion, there are two important objections to be raised against this position. First, and this was one result of our theoretical considerations, if a complete offset for losses is possible, the income tax may reduce the risk of the investor, in spite of the fact that the overall impact is ambiguous. Second - and perhaps more important - an increase in the sales taxes may be disadvantageous because the effect of additional sales taxes is not as clear as is often claimed. If the consumers decrease their demand when additional taxes are imposed on consumer goods, the sales tax has to be paid by the supply side. And the increasing uncertainty of the consumers' reaction will increase the risk connected with the investment.

Putting both objections together, one can conclude that it would better to improve the possibilities to offset losses than to increase sales taxes

II Discrimination against non-innovative investment

The second result of our theoretical considerations was the realization that it may be useful to improve innovative investment by the discrimination of those investments which do not appear to be innovative. This indirect method may be very important for the FRG, because in reality the opposite policy has been pursued in the past. This - in respect to the innovation goal - rather bad situation was revealed in the last "Report on Economic Structure" by the Deutsches Institut für Wirtschaftsforschung, DIW, (German Institute for Economic Research). The report shows that primarily the traditional branches were being supported by tax preferences and direct subsidies whereas more innovative branches were relatively discriminated against. An analysis of the targets of the subvention policy in the FRG makes clear, that - even in 1982 - more than 50 % of those expenditures and tax preferences were used for traditional industries and for (construction of) housing. Only 8 % of the subsidies were given for the improvement of research, information systems and the direct participation of the government in risk.

In my view the most urgent task towards improving innovative investment should be the abolishment of discriminating subsidies and tax preferences.

D Effects of Taxation on the Financing of Investments

I Effects on the supply of funds

From the supply-side view the thesis has been formulated that the deficit in investment in Germany has been partly due to a lack of savings, which arose during the last ten years in the FRG. I agree with this view in respect to the savings of private households for three reasons:

1. During the last ten years the savings of the private households have increased, but not enough to compensate the negative savings of the government and housing sector.

2. The remaining part of the savings of private households has been used mainly for investments in housing instead of for productive purposes.

3. It seems certain that the amount of capital needed to equip industrial work-places will increase further in the future. So the overall rate of savings in the economy also has to increase considerably.

This lack of savings is due in part to the nature of the German income-tax, in particular 3 characteristics: the tax progression rate, the structure of the tax base and tax preferences to stimulate housing.

The slope of the tax rate of the German income-tax shows a high progression in its medium part, where most tax payers are situated. So the progressive rates tax especially the additional income of those persons, who should be able to save relatively more. In spite of frequently repeated political criticism, this unfavourable tariff structure has not been changed. Actually it seems as if the reform of the tariff under discussion may be worsen the problem, because the proposals are

dominated by the goal of relieving families. Such allow-
ances may be important, but should not take priority over
the needed tariff reform.

The structure of the income tax base discriminates
against investment in productive capital, because there
are many preferences for housing purposes only. One could
say that actually these preferences are the only chance
for the lower and middle income classes to build up
wealth. The result are sizeable disallocations in the
housing market, whereas the financing of employment
suffered from a deficit in risk-bearing capital.

II Effects on the risk structure

In comparison to international standards, German firms
suffer from a lack of risk-bearing capital (the quota is
on the average lower than 30 % of total capital). The
system of taxation has supported this development mainly
by the double burden of the wealth tax for corporations,
the different rules of appreciation for different forms
of wealth, and the unequal burden on owned and borrowed
capital caused by the Gewerbesteuer, as well as the
taxation of the emission of additional shares on the
capital market (Gesellschaftsstruktur).

Most important are the problems of wealth taxation. As
German law assumes a greater ability to pay for wealth
owning corporations, their wealth underlies a double
taxation: on the one hand as the wealth of the
corporation itself, on the other hand as the wealth of
the shareholders. Consequently potential shareholders are
reluctant to buy shares, the cost of risk-bearing capital
increases and the corporations prefer to borrow capital
from the banks. Therefore, the minimum essential reform
of the wealth-tax should include a tax relief for
additionally emitted new shares, especially for new
firms.

Besides these problems of mobilizing new risk-bearing capital from outside the firms, there are several proposals to give tax preferences for the self-financing instruments of the firms. To the extent that the loss offset will be improved by these proposals, I agree with them. But as far as they discriminate against financing from outside I am rather sceptical. For in addition to the allocative aspect of the problem, one should keep in mind the distribution problems which will increase in the future. Because the technical revolution we are now facing will reduce the share of labor and the number of workers needed for the production of industrial goods, one of the most important problems is the participation of workers in the ownership of productive capital. Tax policy should be devoted seriously to this target.

Estimation of the Economic Impact of New Technologies on Employment and Productivity

Dieter Friedrich

Introduction

Currently, there is renewed public concern that technological progress, and in particular the recent advances
in automation and information technologies may lead to
increasing structural unemployment. In the current
political discussion, especially in the Federal Republic
of Germany, these problems are combined with the proposal
to reduce the weekly working hours or (and) the amount of
spent working in a life time. Many of the arguments about
the expected economic effects are dependent on the
uncertain future development of productivity.

It is, of course, very difficult to predict with any
certainty the total short-term and long-term employment
and productivity effects of technological changes,
especially as technological progress is only one of the
relevant economic variables. On the one hand, the
discussion in this field becomes emotional. On the other
hand, there is a lot of research and economic studies to
predict the consequences which micro-electronics, robotics, and information technologies will have on jobs.
Most of the contributions concerning the effects of new
technologies (for example micro-electronics, office
automation, computing, telecommunication etc.) are de-
scriptive and qualtitative and do not use the available
tools of economic theory. Although a theoretical foundation and quantification of expected effects on production, income, demand, and price relations is difficult, a
formalized quantitative treatment of the problems may be
helpful for the transparency of the implied assumptions
and can rationalize the discussions.

This contribution is concerned with the impacts of the new technologies on the production process. The effects will be discussed in relation to an extended treatment of technical progress in a traditional production function approach to economic theory.

1. Effects of changes in technology

The term technological progress corresponds broadly to the division in the economic literature between 'macro-economic' studies, which attempt to quantify the rate of technological progress as a function of the growth of output, and 'micro' oriented studies which seek to explain the process of technological change in firms and industries. In this context the knowledge-creating activities of research, invention and development together with the process of absorbtion of new technologies into the productive system are considered. Under economic viewpoints technological progress consists not only of advances in knowledge, but is the result of

- substitution of capital for labor,
- economies of scale,
- learning by doing,
- increased education,
- shifts in resources, and
- organizational improvements.

Before starting the theoretical analysis, some character-istics of the new technologies should be mentioned. As the microelectronics-based technologies open new pros-pects for a rapid evolution of equipment used for receiving, processing, transmitting and acting upon information, microelectronics can said to be a new technological basis for industrial production, an innova-tion comparable, for example, with the introduction of electricity. Three dimensions of the new technology are remarkable, i.e.:

- miniaturization of electronic equipment
  and installation,
- adding 'intelligence' to equipment, and
- rapid processing and transmission of very
  large quantities of information at small cost.

It is broadly accepted that an increased diffusion of microelectronic-based technologies can considerably increase the productivity of the primary input factors labor, capital and material resources by use of

- numerically controlled tools and machines,
- industrial robots,
- computer-aided design and manufacturing,
- flexible manufacturing techniques,
- new organizational structures and computer-
  mediated administration.

Especially the labor productivity of many service sector occupations is being improved by computer systems which allow a possible 'industrialization' of services with a rapid displacement of clerical work. In some jobs, the word decision no longer implies an act of human judgement, but an information processing activity that occurs according to roles implied in an computer program. Computer-mediated work will make it desirable to rethink certain traditional ideas about the nature of organizations and the functions of administration, supervision and control.

There are many reports which contain more detailed descriptions of recent and expected future advances from new technologies primarily based on the advances in microelectronics. However, to overcome a certain lack in formalisation, quantification and in a theoretical underpinning based on economic production theory, we will center this economic analysis on several important effects expected from the new technologies, i.e.:

- substitution of capital for labor in the
  production process in the form of displacement
  of employees and the reduction of working hours,
- embodiment of new technologies in the capital
  stock through new investment,
- changes and improvements in the organization
  and the administrative structure
  (induced by information technologies).

These effects will be specified and measured using classical production theory as a tool. Their influences on the development of (macroelectronic) labor productivity will be analysed both theoretically and empirically.

2. Specification of a production function with regard to new technologies

2.1 Organization of the production process

The speed of access, retrieval, and information processing is allegedly the key to improving the productivity of an organization, but few organizations have seriously considered an appropriate definition of organizational and management productivity in their own operation. Usually, studies on technical progress do not include the structure of organizations. However, induced by communication techniques, improvements in this field can no longer be ignored. We will drop the assumption of the homogeneity of the productive labor input in the production process with respect to the organizational structure.

The organizational structure of firms has been studied by economists, operation analysts, and sociologists, each from a different perspective. Economic studies, such as those by Beckmann (1977, 1983), Calvo/Wellitz, Williamson, Correa and others, pay special attention to the hierarchical structure of firms in relation to different levels of responsibility, different levels of salaries, the optimal and efficient size of the organization, measurement of the management's productivity etc. Here, the approach by M. Beckmann is modified with respect to a hierarchically structured organization with progress in its efficiency. Both the theoretical and the empirical implications of progress in the efficiency of the organizational structure of the production process can be analysed.

We will consider a representative production firm with a well-defined organization with several administrative levels $r=0,1,2,\ldots,R$. R denotes the presidential or top level. Let $r=0$ be the level of the production workers or operatives. The output y_r of management, instruction, supervision and control at level r is the input for the next lower level $r-1$. y_r is produced using the supervision input y_{r-1} from $r+1$ and labor input x_r from level r. We specify the production function for the management and administration outputs y_r to be a Cobb-Douglas function:

$$(2.1) \quad y_r = c_{r+1} \, x_r^a \, y_{r+1}^b \, , \qquad r=0,1,2,\ldots,R-1.$$

The output elasticities a and b of the production function (2.1) are the same at all administrative levels. At the top level $y_R = x_R$ is assumed. Output y_r and the labor input x_r may be interpreted as labor in efficiency units, where $x_r(t) = e^{\gamma_r t} h \Theta_r L_r$ at time t is taken as a product of working hours h, the number L_r of employees at level r, efficiency progress $e^{\gamma_r t}$ with a constant growth rate γ_r, and an efficiency or utilization parameter Θ_r. At level r a part of working hours $h-h_r$ is controlled by the level $r+1$, an other part h_r, in which labor input is not supervised, remains for its own dispositions and for the supervision of the next lower level $r-1$. The efficiency of the uncontrolled working hours h_r may vary, for example, depending on the wage rate w_r, the total capacity utilization of the firm, or the total working hours h. Thus, the constant Θ_r, $0 < \Theta_r < 1$, $r = 1, 2, \ldots, R-1$, $\Theta_0 = 1$, $\Theta_R = 1$ may be conceived as a parameter of the capacity or efficiency utilization of the administration.

At the lowest, operative level, the function for the production of the output Q is assumed to be of the Cobb-Douglas type:

$$(2.2) \quad Q = c_0 \, z^{\alpha} \, y_0^{\beta}$$

z denotes capital input. Details of the structure and the composition of the capital input will be considered in the next section. y_0 is labor input in efficiency units containing the number L_0 of operative workers. Only the employees L_0 at the lowest hierarchical level perform manual labor. The work done by employees at higher levels is entirely administrative (i.e. management, selling, planning, forecasting, supervising, controlling, accounting etc.)

After substitution from (2.1) and (2.2) one obtains

$$(2.3) \quad Q = c \, z^{\alpha} \, \prod_{r=0}^{R-1} x_r^{a\beta b^r} \, x_R \, ,$$

where

$$c = c_0 \prod_{r=1}^{R} c_r^{\beta b^{r-1}}$$

holds. Technical progress is assumed to increase the efficiency of the organization, augmenting the efficiency of the labor input $x_r = e^{\gamma_r t} h^{\Theta_r} L_r$ of the organization. The number R of the administrative levels may only change in the very long run, and is taken here to be constant. Of course, this production function is labor-saving for clerical work.

In the short run, only the labor input L_0 at the operative level $r=0$ can be changed. In a medium range of time, the organization can change staff inputs L_r at all levels $r=1,2,\ldots,R-1$ except the presidential or entrepreneurial level R. Let us show what happens if the labor input changes with technical progress.

a) Let $x^*_r = e^{\gamma_r t} h\Theta_r L^*_r$ be an old and $x_r = e^{\gamma_r t}\Theta_r L_r$ a new quantity of labor input associated with the output levels Q^* and Q. The production function after variation of the operative labor and of the staffs $r=1,2,\ldots,R-1$ output becomes:

$$(2.4) \quad Q = Q^* \prod_{r=0}^{R-1} (x_r/x^*_r)^{a\beta_b{}^r} (x_R/x^*_R)$$

$$= Q^* \prod_{r=0}^{R-1} (L_r/L^*_r)^{a\beta_b{}^r} (L_R/L^*_R),$$

and its cost is

$$(2.5) \quad C = C^* \sum_{r=0}^{R-1} w_r(L_r - L^*_r) = F + \sum_{r=0}^{R-1} w_r L_r.$$

F denotes fixed cost, w_r denotes the wage rate at level r. The president's compensation is assumed to be dependent on profit. For a given output Q and for fixed wages $w_r, r=0,1,2,\ldots,R-1$ we minimize cost.

Form the Lagrangi·an

$$(2.6) \quad F + \sum_{r=0}^{R-1} w_r L_r + \lambda \left[Q - Q^* \prod_{r=0}^{R-1} (L_r/L^*_r)^{a\beta_b{}^r} (L_R/L^*_R) \right]$$

differentiation with respect to L_r yields

$$(2.7) \quad w_r - \lambda Q^* \prod_{i=0}^{R-1} (L_i/L_i^*)^{a\beta b^r} (L_R/L_R^*) (a\beta b^r/L_r) = 0$$

After substitution of the production function (2.4) and after rearrangement one obtains

$$(2.8) \quad w_r = \lambda Q (a\beta b^r / L_r)$$

$$W_r = w_r L_r = \lambda Q a\beta b^r.$$

For a given output Q the wage sum $W_r = w_r L_r$ paid at level r is constant and independent of technical progress. At a given output Q and Θ_r are assumed to be constant, the labor-saving technical progress reduces the quantity $h L_r$ of physical labor input at a constant level $x_r = e^{\gamma_r t} h \Theta_r L_r$ of labor input efficiency. As $W_r = w_r \cdot L_r$ = constant holds, higher efficiency decreases the demand for staff labor input L_r, r=1,2,...,R-1 at increasing wages w_r. Displacements of the white collar jobs with an increasing wage for the remaining highly skilled employees may result.[1]

The displacement effect shows the necessity for individual education, re-education and training for highly skilled workers. In a pessimistic view, one may also reduce an increasing income discrepancy between employed and unemployed white collar workers for the future.

b) A shortage of weekly labor hours may increase the parameter Θ_r and not reduce the efficiency of the organizations, since an invariant product $h\Theta_r$ can be supposed. From the view of the administrative process this can be attained by an increase in utilization of idle organizational capacities leading to a higher efficiency of clerical work. New technologies such as office automation, word processing, information techniques (telematics, telecommunication, remote supervision etc.) may additionally support the capacity $h\Theta_r$ assumed to be constant. As a result of the reduction in working hours the inducement to hire new more highly skilled clerical workers at a higher administrative level may be scarce, and employment impulses for the administrative level will be compensated by the advance in new information technologies.

c) The change in staff input at all levels of the organization in a medium range of time may occur according to the natural departure of older employees. This will worsen the situation for young persons (academically skilled) beginning work and considerably reduce the chance to find a job in an organization staff. Furthermore, an additional reduction in the time spent working in one's lifetime can be expected to facilitate and accelerate the speed of staff reorganization without an equivalent increase in the demand for traditionally educated white-collar employees without skills in computer-mediated work.

2.2 Production at the operative level

In the last section the production function (2.2) at the operative level $r=0$ is assumed to be of a simple Cobb-Douglas type with homogenous capital input. In a more realistic view the composition and the utilization of the capital stock should be taken into account.

From the specification (2.1) and (2.2) one obtains

$$(2.9) \quad Q = c_0 \, z^\alpha \, y_0^\beta = c_0 \left[\kappa h K\right]^\alpha \left[c_1 (e^{\gamma_0 t} \, h\Theta_0 \, L_0)^a \, y_1^b\right]^\beta,$$

$$\Theta_0 = 1,$$

where capital input z is written as $z = h K$ and $y_0 = c_1 (e^{\gamma_0 t} h\Theta_0 L_0)^a y_1^b$ hold. The capital input flow is defined as a product of capital stock K and the time h of working hours. The parameter $\kappa (0 < \kappa < 1)$ denotes the degree of capacity utilization.

To pay more attention to the composition of the capital stock two types of capital goods will be distinguished, each with a different amount of increase in technical progress and productivity, i.e.

- equipment, tools and machinery (denotes as K_1), and
- buildings and plants (denoted as K_2).

Introducing the different capital stocks in the production function we have after rearrangement

$$(2.10) \quad Q = c_0 \; c_1^{\beta} \; e^{a\beta\gamma_0 t} \; (\kappa h \; K_1)^{\alpha_1} \; (h \; K_2)^{\alpha_2} \; (hL_0)^{a\beta} \; y_1^{b\beta}$$

with the corresponding output elasticities α_1 and α_2.

Improvements through new microelectronics-based technologies require new investments in equipment. Therefore, the use of new technologies at the operative production level can be considered as an embodiment of technical progress, incorporated in new investments. Assuming that the production function shifts upward over time, the new capital depends upon the design of the new machinery and the year-of-production-effect associated with time. When the improvements in embodied technology permits the quantity of new machines to improve with the rate λ_1 we have

$$(2.11) \quad K_1(t) = \int_{-\infty}^{t} e^{\lambda_1 v} \; M_v(t) \; dv,$$

where

$$(2.12) \quad M_v(t) = e^{-\delta_1(t-v)} I_1(v)$$

denotes the gross amount of investment in the year v (of the year of production v) which is still in use at time t. $I_1(v)$ is the gross investment in machinery in the year v. δ_1 denotes the rate of depreciation with no allowance for decreasing efficiency.

In an equivalent manner we get for the capital stock of plants and of buildings the expression

$$(2.14) \quad K_2(t) = e^{-\delta_2 t} \int_{-\infty}^{t} e^{(\delta_2 + \lambda_2)v} I_2(v) \, dv,$$

where $I_2(v)$ denotes gross investment in buildings in the year v, λ_2 is the rate of technical change, and δ_2 denotes the corresponding depreciation rate.

After substitution of the capital years of production in the production function (2.10) we obtain

$$(2.15) \quad Q = c_0 \; c_1^\beta \; e^{\phi_0 t} \; h^{\phi_3} \; (\kappa \int_{-\infty}^{t} e^{\phi_1 v} I_1(v) \, dv)^{\alpha_1}$$

$$(\int_{-\infty}^{t} e^{\phi_2 v} I_2(v) \, dv)^{\alpha_2} \; L_0^{a\beta} \; y_1^{b\beta} ,$$

where

$$\phi = a\beta\gamma_0 - \alpha_1\delta_1 - \alpha_2\delta_2$$

$$\phi = (\delta_1 + \lambda_1)$$

$$\phi = (\delta_2 + \lambda_2)$$

$$\phi = \alpha_1 + \alpha_2 + a\beta$$

hold.

2.3 Capital utilization and working hours

A variation in the capacity utilization changes the flow of capital input. In the specification (2.9) of the production function a decrease in the capacity utilization will lower the employment of all machinery in the same way. However, in the year of production approach, the machines of various years of production have differing productivity, where new equipment is assumed to contain the modern technologies with the highest productivity. When overall capacity utilization decreases, we can expect that firms prefer to use the capital goods with the highest productivity, and will first reduce the use of older machines. To take the differences in productivity into account, we write for the rate of capacity utilization:

$$(2.16) \quad \kappa = \frac{\int_{t-J}^{t} e^{-\delta_1(t-v)} I_1(v) \, dv}{\int_{-\infty}^{t} e^{-\delta_1(t-v)} I_1(v) \, dv}$$

J denotes the year of fabrication of the oldest machine in use, and changes with the variation of the capacity utilization. It should be clear that a reduction in the production level, associated with a reduced capacity utilization, will increase the productivity. Therefore, high productivity at a low production level will accelerate the problem of unemployment in a business cycle recession. Therefore, the new technology can be said to produce pro-cyclical employments effects.

For a modification of the production function with respect to differences in the productivity of machines of various years of production, one obtains from the solution of the integral equation (2.16) the variable J, depending on the actual level of the capacity utilization κ. In the production function (2.15) the capital stock for equipment and machinery in use may be written as:

$$(2.17) \quad \int_{t-J}^{t} e^{\phi_1 v} I_1(v) \, dv \ .$$

Furthermore, the intensity of capital utilization depends

on the working hours h. The problems of the reduction of working hours should be discussed in relation with the utilization of the capital stock. Here, we can consider two extreme situations:

a) Lowering the number of working hours may reduce the labor input and the capital input in the same way. In this case, the labor productivity per hour, expressed as Q/hL_0 may not significantly change. However, the capital productivity, usually written as Q/K, will be reduced considerably. Lowering the utilization of the capital stock in the same way as working hours h, we require a higher stock of capital to keep up the same level Q of production. A reduction of the capital input flow Kh occurs simultaneously with h. As L_0h is assumed to be constant, we may expect $L_0h = (h-\Delta h)(L_0+\Delta L_0)$ for a positive employment effect ΔL_0. Introducing working hours into the production function, capital and labor become limitational input factors. An additional employment effect may be attained by an expansion of the capacity utilization, i.e. an increase in κ or J. However, the additional use of older equipment will slightly lower the labor productivity per hour. In a first approach, the recent degree of capital utilization i.e. the additional occupation of the idle capital stock will cause an additional employment effect. [2]

b) In a second manner, the reduction of working hours may be combined with an expansion of the capital utilization. This may be attained by a more flexible organization. For example, in the production function we consider an additional employment of labor ΔL_0. However, as time is a limitational factor in the production process, we assume job-sharing, where L_0 and ΔL_0 use the same capital equipment, but not at the same working hours. L_0 can be assumed as day shift, and ΔL_0 may be introduced as 'night shift', thus, both use the same stock of capital at different times. Under this assumption, the production function yields:

$$(2.18) \quad Q = c_0 \; c_1^{\beta} \; e^{a\beta\gamma_0 t} \left[\kappa(h+\Delta h_K)K_1 \right]^{\alpha_1} \left[(h+\Delta h_K)K_2 \right]^{\alpha_2}$$
$$h(L_0+\Delta L_0)^{a\beta} \; y_1^{b\beta}.$$

From an additional use of capital denoted as $\Delta h_K K$, a higher capital productivity Q/K may result. As working time is a limitational factor in the production process, the propositions for the reduction of working hours should not be discussed without regard to the problems of capital utilization and a higher flexibility for the organization of working hours. In this case, the reduction of working hours can be combined with an increase in the productivity of capital.

3. Empirical results

For the estimation of the production relation we take R = 3 and distinguish four kinds of labor inputs. i.e.:

L_0: blue collar workers, employed in production
    and transportation,
L_1: blue collar workers, employed in control,
    maintenance, repair and other services,
L_2: white collar employees (without
    top management functions),
L_3: entrepreneurs and employees at the top
    management level.

For the FRG only time series for the number L_0+L_1 (i.e. 'Arbeiter') are available. From the cross-section (Mikrozensus) we have figures for the ratio $r_{0/1} = L_0/(L_0+L_1)*100$ (for example, in 1969: 64.1 % and in 1979: 57.6 %). An average ratio depending on time can be estimated, obtaining $r_{0/1} = 69.96 \; e^{-0.00972(j-1960)}$ for the years j=1960,1961,.... The number L_3 consists of the group of entrepreneurs ('Selbständige') and the number of employees with management functions. From cross-section data (Mikrozensus) we have figures for the estimation of an average ratio of white collar employees occupied at the management level (for example, in 1969: 10.8 % and in 1979: 9.6 % of the employees have a management occupation). A relation $r_{2/3} =$ 11.893 $e^{-0.01071(j-1960)}$ can be obtained, giving the ratio of top level employees for the years j=1960,1961,...

Combining the specification elements for the production function with an organizational structure with four levels r=0,1,2,3 of organization staff one obtains:

$$(3.1) \quad Q = c \, e^{\gamma_0 t} \, (h \, K_1)^{\alpha_1} \, (h \, K_2)^{\alpha_2} \, L^{\beta},$$

where

$$(3.2) \quad K_1 = \int_{t-J}^{t} e^{\phi_1 v} \, I_1(v) \, dv,$$

$$(3.3) \quad K_2 = \int_{-\infty}^{t} e^{\phi_2 v} \, I_2(v) \, dv,$$

$$(3.4) \quad L = (h \, L_0)^{a} \, (h \Theta L_1)^{ab} \, (h \Theta L_2)^{ab^2} \, (h \, L_3)^{b^3}$$

hold. The compositions of the parameters are defined as:

$$\phi_0 = (a + ab + ab^2 + b^3) \, \beta\gamma - \alpha_1\delta_1 - \alpha_2\delta_2$$
$$\phi_1 = (\delta_1 + \lambda_1)$$
$$\phi_2 = (\delta_2 + \lambda_2)$$

γ, λ_1 and λ_2 denote the rates of technical progress for labor input, equipment and buildings respectively. δ_1 and δ_2 give the rate of depreciation for machinery and buildings. The other parameters denote the wellknown production elasticities for the Cobb-Douglas function.

Production functions for the sectors

- energy and mining,
- manufacturing,

- building constructing,
- trade,
- traffic and information transmission,
- banking and insurance, and
- other services

have been estimated for the Federal Republic of Germany.

We will discuss the most important and interesting result for industrial manufacturing. From seasonally adjusted quarterly data for the years 1970 to 1981 we have the following estimates:

$$
\begin{array}{lll}
\phi_0 = -0.032291 & \alpha_1 = 0.56479 & a = 0.073509 \\
\phi_1 = 0.094792 & \alpha_2 = 0.29687 & b = 0.498796 \\
\phi_2 = 0.045538 & \beta = 0.35477 & c = 1.145952 \\
\end{array}
$$

$$
\begin{array}{ll}
R^2 = 0.9500 & \rho = 0.95127 \\
\sigma_u = 1.6472 &
\end{array}
$$

In the Cobb-Douglas function the parameter h, indicating working hours, has the same effect as a scale factor, i.e. all input factors will be multiplied with the same factor of working hours. After rearrangement of the production function we can write the scale factor h as a separable input factor:

$$(3.5) \quad Q = c \; e^{\phi_0 t} \; h^\rho \; L_0^a \; (\Theta L_1)^{ab} \; (\Theta L_2)^{ab^2} \; L_3^{b^3}.$$

The exponent of the parameter h can be written as

$$\rho = (a + ab + ab^2 + b^3)\,\beta\gamma - \alpha_1\delta_1 - \alpha_2\delta_2 = 0.9512$$

denoting the elasticity of scale. This parameter may indicate constant ($\rho = 1$), increasing ($\rho > 1$) or decreasing ($\rho < 1$) economies of scale for the input variation of the production of the manufacturing sector. Because the elasticity

$$(3.6) \quad \frac{\partial \ln Q}{\partial \ln h} = \frac{Q}{h} \frac{\partial h}{\partial Q} = 0.9512$$

of scale is less than unity, a reduction of the working hours by 1 % be associated with a decrease in the output only by 0.95 %. Furthermore, shortening working hours will simultaneously change the labor productivity per hour, defined as Q/Lh. From the Cobb-Douglas production function one obtains the elasticity

$$(3.7) \quad \frac{\partial \ln(Q/Lh)}{\partial \ln(h)} = \rho - 1 = -0.05$$

for the labor productivity with respect of the variation of working hours. Only in the case of constant returns to scale will this elasticity be zero. In the case of $\rho = 0.95$, associated with decreasing returns to scale, a shortage of working hours will simultaneously increase labor productivity and may stimulate trade unions to claim the redistribution of the increase in productivity. For an identification of the rate γ technical progress which is incorporated in labor we require prior information about the rates of depreciation for equipment and buildings. In the meaningful range of the depreciation rates the labor progress rate varies as follows:

δ_1 %	δ_2 %	γ %
5.2	1.15	0.6
5.3	1.20	1.3
5.4	1.25	2.1
5.5	1.30	3.7
5.6	1.35	4.5
5.5	1.30	2.9
5.6	1.35	3.7
5.7	1.40	4.5
5.8	1.45	5.3
5.9	1.50	6.1
6.0	1.55	6.9

For convenient depreciation rates we can suppose that the technical progress associated with the labor input varies between three and six percent. The labor combined progress rate is higher than the rate for progress incorporated in capital. Therefore, the estimates show a biased, more labor-saving technical progress.

The importance of the organization structure can be taken from the input elasticities a, b and β of the labor inputs. For the manufacturing sector the elasticity of the labor input L_0 at the lowest level is very small. We have

$$a\beta = \frac{\partial(\ln Q)}{\partial(\ln L_0)} = 0.073509 \cdot 0.35477 = 0.026078.$$

The dominant role of highly skilled labor input becomes evident and shows a typical situation for developed industrial countries, where an increase in productivity depends mainly on the quality of the highly skilled labor input.

On the other hand, a small output elasticity indicates high employment impulses with respect to a small variation in output. However, the substitution and the employment effects can only be consideres in relation to the factor prices. Minimizing cost in production, for marginal products Q_K and Q_L of capital and labor Q_K/Q_L = k/w holds. k and w denote capital cost and wages, respectively. For the Cobb-Douglas production function one obtains, for example,

$$(3.8) \quad \frac{k}{w} = \frac{\alpha_1}{a\beta} \frac{L_0}{K_1}$$

To show the dependence on working hours we assume a shortening of working hours with fully compensated nominal wages, whereby the constant monthly incomes

$m = h \cdot w = h^* \cdot w^*$ before and after the reduction of the working time will be equal. h^* and w^* denote working hours and wages after the reduction. Substitution, rearrangement and differentiation with respect to time yields

$$(3.9) \quad L_0 = \frac{a\beta}{\alpha_1} \frac{k}{m} h K_1$$

and

$$(3.10) \quad \dot{L}_0 = \frac{a\beta}{\alpha_1} \frac{k}{m} (\dot{h} K_1 + h \dot{K}_1).$$

A reduction $\dot{h} < 0$ in working hours will lower the number of employees at all levels, depending upon the elasticity of production. Here, the high elasticity of staff employees input indicates future labor market problems due to the new information technologies. The higher the elasticity, the higher the reduction of substitution. Note that positive impulses for employment result not from the reduction in working hours, but from the investment ($I = \dot{K}$), associated with the substitution from labor to capital.

4. Concluding remarks

This paper shows some of the difficulties in the measurement of production relations and productivity, when considering working hours in the production process. A lot of economic questions can only be answered if we determine how productivity will be changed. A reduction in working time alters simultaneously the labor productivity. The effect depends upon the returns to scale. Attention must be given to the problems of capital utilization and of flexibility in job sharing. Furthermore, in economic production theory the organizational structure should be taken into account, because new information technologies will affect the administration

and the organization of work at all administrative
levels. This approach from neoclassical production theory
shows only some aspects of the supply side and ignores
macroeconomic interdependencies. These studies must be
completed by demand analyses, because simultan effects
can only be demonstrated in an interdependent demand and
supply model.

Footnotes:

(1) However, compensation effects on the macroeconomic
     level, for example, the creation of new jobs for
     programmers, computer operators, software engineers
     etc., and wage pressure from the supply side of the
     labor market should be taken into account.

(2) Otherwise we must assume that the labor $h(L_0 + \Delta L_0)$
     can increase output at a constant available capital
     stock. In this case, the actual combination of
     capital and labor is not efficient and the firms
     have not attained the minimization of cost.

References

BECKMANN, M. J. (1977): Production Functions and the
     Theory of the Firm. Journal of Economic Theory, Vol.
     14, pp. 1-18.

BECKMANN, M. J. (1978): Rank in Organizations. Lecture
     Notes in Economics and Mathematical Systems, No.
     161, Berlin/Heidelberg/New York.

BECKMANN, M. J. (1983): Production Functions in the
     Analysis of Organizational Structure, in: SATO, R.;
     BECKMANN, M. J. (Editors): Technology, Organization
     and Economic Structure. Essays in Honor of Prof.
     Isamu Yamada. Lecture Notes in Economics and
     Mathematical Systems. Berlin/Heidelberg/New York, p.
     2-14.

BLAU, P. M. (1976): Technology and Organization in
     Manufacturing. Administrative Sciences Quarterly,
     Vol. 21, p. 20-40.

BMFT (1980): Bundesministerium für Forschung und Techno-
     logie. Schriftenreihe Technologie und Beschäftigung,
     Band 1: Neue Technologie und Beschäftigung. Düssel-
     dorf 1980. Band 2: Technischer Fortschritt -
     Auswirkungen auf Wirtschaft und Arbeitsmarkt. Düs-
     seldorf 1980.

BOCHUM, H. (1976): Choice of the Organization Structure: A Framework for Quantitative Analysis of Industrial Centralization / Decentralization in Manufacturing Issues. Zeitschrift für Operations Research, Vol. 20, B17-B35.

CALVO, A. G.; WELLISZ, S. (1978): Supervision, Loss of Control, and the Optimum Size of the Firm., Journal of the Political Economy, Vol. 86, p. 943-952.

CHINLOY, P. (1981): Labor Productivity. Cambridge Massachusetts (Abt Books).

CORREA, H. (1983): Firm's Administrative Structure: Theory, Measurement and Application to Growth Accounting and Income Distribution. Empirical Economics, Vol. 8, p. 93-109.

GIJSEL, de P. (1983): Verantwortung und Entlohnung, Frankfurt (Campus) 1983.

GRILICHES, Z.; RINGSTAD, V. (1971): Economies of Scale and the Form of the Production Function. Amsterdam (North Holland).

IFO (1980): Institut fuer Wirtschaftsforschung. Technischer Fortschritt - Auswirkungen auf Wirtschaft und Arbeitsmarkt. Berlin.

KENNEDY, C.; THIRLWALL, A. P. (1972): Surveys in Applied Economics: Technical Progress. Economic Journal, Vol. 82 (325), p. 11-72.

KOCHEM, M. (1973): Decentralization by Function and Location. Management Science, Vol. 19, p. 841-856.

KOCHEM, M.; DEUTSCH, K. W. (1972): Pluralization: A Mathematical Model. Operations Research, Vol. 20, p. 276-292.

NADIRI, M. I. (1970): Some Approaches to the Theory and Measurement of Economic Literature, Vol. 8, p. 1137-1177.

OECD (1982): Micro-electronics, Robotics and Jobs. Information Computer Communication Policy, Paris.

RADA, J. (1980): The impact of Micro-Electronics. ILO, Genf.

SATO, R.; NONO, T. (1983): Invariance Principle and 'G-Neutral' Types of Technical Change, in: SATO, R.; BECKMANN, M. (Editors): Technology, Organization and Economic Structure. Essays in Honor of Prof. Isamu Yamada. Lecture Notes in Economics and Mathematical Systems, No. 210, Berlin/Heidelberg/New York, p. 177-186.

SOLOW, R. M. (1957): Technical Change and the Aggregate Production Function. The Review of Economics and Statistics, Vol. 39, p. 312-320.

STONEMAN, P. (1976): Technological Diffusion and the Computer Revolution. Cambridge (University Press).

WILLIAMSON, O. E. (1967): Hierarchical Control and Optimal Firm Size. The Journal of Political Economy, Vol. 75, p. 123-138.

Flexibility of Work - Scope and Design

Hans-Josef Brink

1. Flexibility in Business Administration and Practice

The term "flexibility" is used with different intentions
in science and practice. This fact holds in the field of
business administration, too. The discussion on flexibility in business administration was not successful in
developing a terminology and a generally accepted concept
of flexibility. This is due less to the complexity of the
empirical phenomenon flexibility, but more to different
research perspectives in analysing such problems.

Business administration traditionally examines aspects of
flexibility within the theories of decision making,
organizations, production and cost.

In the theory of decision-making, flexibility is described as the various possibilities one has to reduce the
risk involved with profits or to improve the certainty of
profits. The planning of flexibility is considered as the
planning of adaptation, in the sense of compensation of
risk. The theory of organization interprets flexibility
as a contingency variable, understood as the capability
to adapt oneself by means of internal modifications to
changes in the environment, or to improve profiting in a
given environment. The concept of "organization development" claims to be able to raise the flexibility and
adaptability of an organization. The ideas on organizational flexibility focus on man and his qualifications
and social adaptability. Today's theory of production and
cost has been influenced by E. Gutenberg. His processes
of operational adjustment may be seen as the realities of
flexibility. Their consequences, expressed in quantities
and values, represent the impact of flexibility decisions. The transformation of these reflections on

production and cost into accounting by means of flexible budgeting represents an analysis of flexibility, too. Production economics interprets flexibility as the capability of a production system to adjust to changes in the qualities and quantities of production, procurement and sales. A distinction is made between the flexibility of the stock, the given potential of the operating resources) and the flexibility of development (the variable potential of the operating resources).

For our further reflections, flexibility will be viewed as a person's ability to act or to work independently of rigid internal or external constraints. Thereby flexibility is considered a capacity to operate relatively autonomously in regard to alternative constellations in the environment. This definition yields the statement that there is no overall flexibility of a subject, but only a constraint-specific flexibility.

The substantial concretization of flexibility requires the specification of the subject. According to our topic, we will analyze the flexibilization of work. The concept "work" includes in German usage activities as well as the results of activities. This traditional view of work will be integrated into the general action approach. This action approach yields foundations for the following reflections on a systematization of the flexibility of work.

2. Elements of Action as Attributes of the Systematization of Flexibility of Work

2.1 Elements of Action

Considerations of work as a factor and as performance mean different interpretations of actions. It seems reasonable to focus on the general view of an action and to use the elements of an action as a starting point for a systematization of the flexibility of work.

Each action can be described by its elements: (1) task
(objective), (2) subject, (3) means, (4) activity, (5)
object, (6) time and (7) space/location. The elements
"time" and "space/locaction" are of accessory character.
Therefore it is useful to distinguish between primary and
secondary specification of action elements. The matrix in
Annex 1 illustrates this view. Each action element of the
primary specification may be further described by the
secondary elements of quantity, quality and space/loca-
tion.

2.2 Flexibilization of Action Elements

The transfer of the concept of flexibility defined above
to action elements opens another dimension (Annex 2).
Flexibility can be divided into three types: (1) in-
flexibility, (2) partial flexibility and (3) total
flexibility. This modification may be illustrated with
regard to materials. An inflexible view means the representation of a certain material by only one quality,
partial flexibility is a representation by classes of
qualities. When one speaks of total flexibility, one
means a distinction of qualities for each lot. Such a
modification of the idea of flexibility can be applied to
work.

The systematization of flexibility according to Annex 2
focuses on organizational units (working systems).
Further types of flexibility may be distinguished (Annex
3). The flexibility of organizational units is part of
the flexibility of the firm.

An analysis of the flexibility of an organizational unit
follows a step-by-step approach. The first step examines
organizational units with regard to the action approach,
the second step investigates the autonomy of action
(Annex 4) of organizational units and thereby their

flexibility. Two methods of flexibility measurement can be applied: On the one hand the enumeration of the constraints satisfied by the unit, on the other hand the enumeration of the scope of actions. A necessary condition for measurement is designating relevant constraints as standards of flexibility. For example, flexibility concerning prices means another category than the flexibility of machines concerning processing of different qualities of material.

3. Flexibilization of Working Time as an Element of the Flexibilization of Work

The discussion on the flexibilization of working time is of great importance in social and economic policy. Today, science and economic practice deal daily with this phenomena. The disputes between employers and trade unions focus on the reduction of working time, while the individual unions prefer different methods of reduction. It is not my intention to examine this discussion more deeply in this lecture, nor will we discuss the vast number of realized models of flexibilization of working time, all dealing with the duration of work and work flow process.

The flexibilization of working time is an instrument for the business entity as well as for the single employee. The term "flexibilization of working time" indicates not a single instrument for adjustment, but a vast complex of instruments. Business practice illustrates this. But there is a gap in the systematization of working time flexibilization. The following reflections should help clear up this problem. Annex 5 lists the relevant dimensions for the description of the duration of working time and work flow process as partial instruments in the flexibilization of working time. This systemization makes possible the recording and classification of models of working time. Two models will serve as examples: Heraeus and teachers in Baden-Württemberg.

W.C. Heraeus GmbH, Hanau, makes monthly agreements on working time and work flow process especially in administration. Former rigid part-time and fulltime work has been replaced by a variety of working time configurations. Individual contracts cover the whole range between 4 and 7 hours per day without a strict requirement to actually work the whole numer of hours contracted every day. Working times are managed with the participation and according to the needs of the employees on the one hand, and the needs of the firm on the other. The stated results are that the employees, organizing their work themselves and introducing their individual wishes, are more content and feel exceptionally responsible for their work. Positive motivation is also indicated by lower absenteeism due to illness and improved performance. The example of flexibilization in this firm illustrated that there is no need to lay off personnel, in spite of a decreased volume of work. Models of making working time more flexible are judged positively on the whole, even if the acceptance of these models hardly reached the production area because of management problems. The working time models of Heraeus will be presented in our scheme.

Because of the unemployment of many teachers, models of working time reduction are being discussed in Baden-Württemberg. These models are characterized by elements such as weekly working time, individual solutions, the legal foundations, self control, medium-term reversibility, limited availability and operating levels.

4. Flexibilization of Working Time as a Problem of Design

The variation of working time in duration and in the work flow process is a multidimensional problem. Traditional approaches emphasize the organizational aspect and neglect the employees view. This approach now seems to be problematic in several aspects. As business practice illustrates, there is a need for flexibility not only by organizations but also by employees. The organizational need for flexibility is caused by changes in input and output markets and by technological innovations. Changes in individual behavior in work and leisure evoke a need for flexibility by the employee concerned. Thus, the aspect of the employees is to be emphasized more than before. Following to these reflections, the design of flexibilization has to fit the organization's and the employees' view, using the element approach. From this complex of elements, the basic structure of possible adjustments in the predicated exogeneous reduction of working time is illustrated (Annex 6). This (surely incomplete) complex contains the instruments of different maturity and adjustment.

The design of adjustment means the selection of adjustment instruments and their execution on the administrative and operational level. Selection postulates an analysis of the effects of the instruments with regard to the objectives and constraints. This analysis is difficult, because of a variety of measurement problems. Concerning the overall statements on the reduction of working time - also made in this seminar - some doubt seems justified if one considers the broad variety of adjustment parameters, and the different profit and market situation of various business entities. One must ask whether plant size influences adjustment policy. One may assume that small and medium-sized firms are much more affected by a reduction in working hours. On the one hand, there is a danger of dislocation between the stock of operating resources and the staff size because of constraints of integers and a jerky increase in capacity through investments. On the other hand, one may presume that many small firms are not in a position powerful enough to capture new markets or to preserve existing markets. Their market position will not allow them to shift increasing costs resulting from reduction of working time on to their customers. From an organizational view, overall or inflexible regulations of working time seem to be very problematic. Another argument for dealing flexibly with working time are the very different needs for flexibility among employees. These needs require flexibility both in time and in perfomance. According to the idea of humanization, emphasized also by the trade unions, one has to look for possibilities to satisfy these needs of the employees. This requires new structures of management and organization and more flexibility in the contract negotiations too. The solution of this complex task necessitates great imagination and an acceptance of responsibility.

Annex 1

Matrix of the Action Approach to Formal Systematization of the Flexibilization of Work

primary specification	secondary specification			
	quantity	quality	time	space/location
objective				
subject				
means				
operations (activity)				
object				
results				

Annex 2

Scope of Flexibilization

formal dimension / substantial dimension	inflexibility (fixed) (one value)	partial flexibility (intermediate values)	total flexibility (individual values)
elements of action			
objective			
subject			
.			
.			
.			
time			
space/location			
performance			

Annex 3

Types of Flexibility

object of reference	kinds of flexibility	
	intra-firm flexibility	inter-firm flexibility
organization (firm)		
organizational unit	intra-unit flexibility (working system flex.)	inter-unit flexibility

Annex 4

Step-by-Step-Conception of Analysis of the Flexibility on an Organizational Unit

1st Step: Analysis of an organizational unit with the assistance of the action approach
- performance of primary specification
- performance of (accessory) secondary specification

2nd Step: Analysis of the action autonomy (flexibility)
- determination of relevant constraints concerning investigations for flexibility
- measurement of flexibility (room to maneuver)
- determination of adaptation speed
- evaluation of flexibility

Annex 5

Flexibilization of Working Time

subjects of design / dimensions	working time duration	working time; work flow process	working time duration and work flow process
1. type of working time – total working time of life – annual working time – monthly working time – weekly working time – daily working time			
2. personnel scope of validity – homogeneous (all employees) – specified by groups – specified by individuals			
3. legal foundation – law – industry-wide collective agreement – plant agreement – individual agreement			
4. decision unit – employer (external control) – employee (self control) – negotiation (participation)			

5. reversibility of working time flexibility
– not reversible
– reversible
  – short-term
  – medium-term (time lag)			

6. time of validity – limited in time – unlimited in time			
7. level – administrative level – operating level			

Annex 6

Morphological Approach to Firm Adaptation to Exogeneous Predicated Reduction of Working Time

attribute	scope of variable		
(1) pricing policy	no shifting of increased costs,		total shifting of increased costs
(2) production program	no change	reduction	liquidation of the company
(3) operating resources	no changes	rationalization measures	automatization
(4) personnel			
– increase in performance	no		long term performance
– extra work	no		maximum duration
– change of staff size	no		hiring (additional shift)
(5) make or buy	buy	mixed	make
(6) location	complete relocation	partial relocation	no relocation

Impact of New Technologies on Personnel Management with Special Reference to Office Automation

Toshio Kanishima

I Introduction

Recently there have been a great number of technological innovations. One of them is the development of computer. For instance, Japan is currently undergoing "The Fifth Generation Computer Development". Thus my contribution to the 8th Seminar is right on time to discuss the characteristics of the new technological innovations and their impact on personnel management through Office Automation (OA). The Japan Institute for Office Automation has made several surveys on the impacts and effects of OA on Japanese business management, and the Japan Society for the Study of Office Automation has also discussed its impacts and effects on Japanese employment and personnel management.

II Computer Development

The personnel management environment in modern enterprises is said to be appropriate for the new era in computers. Needless to say, the core of recent technological innovations is the development of the computer. For instance, the Japanese Ministry for International Trade and Industries, too has already invested the huge amount of 100 billion yen in "The Fifth Generation Computer Development" as a national project. It is widely expected that the MITI project will be successfully accomplished in the near future.

The development of the computer has advanced from the very simple vacuum tube of the first generation to the transistor. Integratic Circuits (IC), and the very

efficient LSI in the second, third and fourth genera-
tions, respectively. The speed and capacity of an
advanced computer is incomparable with the older ones.
Today, efforts are being devoted towards creating
"artificial intelligence" to resemble that of the human
brain. These efforts are without doubt also based on the
recent technological innovations in the field of electronics.

Moreover, the plan to develop an Information Network
System (INS) by the Nippon Telegraph and Telephone Public
Corporation will sooner or later also lead to changes in
the business world, approaching that which one can call
"a high-speed communication" society.

III Characteristics of New Technological Innovations

W.W. Rostow describes the present technological innovation as "The Fourth Industrial Revolution". The first
innovation took place in England during the 1780s, when
new methods of iron manufacturing were invented and the
mass production of thread and yarns was started. The
second era of innovation occurred in America during the
1870s, when the railroad and steel revolution took place.
The third then began around the turn of the century,
lasting up until 1960 when electricity, new chemical
substances and the internal combustion engine played
important roles. Now the fourth technological innovation
has come, consisting of microelectronics (ME), communication systems, biotechnology, laser-beams, robots and new
synthetic materials etc. They are preparing the way for a
new phase of innovation which will probably develop
beyond our imaginations. The following three features
will sufficiently characterize the present innovation:
firstly, it is principally based on advanced knowledge of
various basic sciences. Secondly, the fields of application range widely from basic to service industries and
from medical care to education. Thirdly, it is of

international relevance in the sense that it affects not only developed but also developing countries.

IV Office Automation and Changes in Personnel Management

The changes induced in personnel management by the innovation can be differentiated into the rationalization of office management, in other words OA (Office Automation) and the rationalization of factory management or FA (Factory Automation).

It is generally known that modern enterprises introducing OA systems apply personal computers and word processors in order to edit graphs or accounting statements, documents etc., and make use of them also for electronic-mail services, dictation, receipts and files collection, image-data processing and conferences. All these practices will be offered on a commercial basis sooner or later. This is of course carried on through technological innovations. That is to say, first a Local Area Network (LAN) system that is required as a new infrastructure. Secondly, the establishment of office information networks to do efficient allotting and assembling of inter-office information is required. Lastly, the invention of man-machine interfacing or the establishment of work stations in offices is neccessary.

The aforementioned new general purpose computer system that has OA as its main application may entail problems that probably detract from our primary goal. It is neccessary therefore to find a reconciliation between such data processing and OA itself. Accordingly, it is exceedingly urgent to establish an integrated office system from each piece of multimedia equipment connected to the OA machinery. It goes without saying that these series of super computers, word processors (both mono or bi-lingual), personal computers cannot as such be operated efficiently without the rationalization of human resource development within the enterprise concerned.

It is true that technological innovation itself brings about new materials as well as the other advancements mentioned above. It provokes new problems such as inter-national trade friction, disputes over military build-up and industrial spionage cases, all of which are unfavor-able to all concerned. This implies that we need the new computer system which has the human aspect as its vital aspect, and in which the interface between communication and computer neccessarily has the human factor as its main guiding principle. This will without fail make personnel management a topic deserving avid attention.

V Micro-Electronics and Health Discorders

During a sluggish economic situation with a low growth rate, personnel management and employment are particular-ly affected. Investigations by the Center for Recruitment during the job-search season indicate an improvement in the situation for female student graduates, while unskilled labor is being replaced by mechanization. Moreover, there is much potential for female labor in the service sector. All these facts imply that only those who are highly capable are being employed by the enterprises. The report by the Ministry of Labor on micro-electronics (ME) and labor planning indicates that the orientation towards ME requires high technical proficiency hence resulting in a necessity for adaptability from the middleaged laborers. The higher the tendency towards use of ME, the greater the level of concentration, the less work there will be available for sub-contractors. And finally, new tension in labor relations is created, as firms tend to orient themselves more and more towards ME.

Concerning personnel management, the Ministry adds that the introduction of robots, OA (in 1975), and especially ME brought about problems in those types of industries with a typically Japanese style of management. They are also those which are not able to adapt themselves to the rapid changes in technological innovation.

Concerning work-related disease and the revolution in OA, here the studies by the Labor Research Institute point to physical disorders characterized by complex symptoms and chronic ills. This means that abrupt advances in technical innovation go hand in hand with invironmental changes for personnel management and for the work-place. Other health disorders caused by alienation of human beings towards machines and machinery range, for instance, from arm-paralysis, buzzing in the ears, headaches, visual problems, shoulder stipness, and nervous breakdowns, to feeling abnormally cold in one's feet, insufficient exercise etc. All these need to be voiced strongly now in the age of ME where the worker's personal worth and dignity should be maintained. Especially, the problems felt by female workers must be considered when introducing OA systems, and counter measures undertaken. For example, the move towards the "on-line" system and the proportional introduction of machinery as part of office rationalization will from time to time create problems. The employers' solutions are perhaps reshuffling workers, a system of shorter terms of employment, etc., until another solution to unemployment is found.

VI Human Resource Development and Management Once Again

Firms with a Japanese-style employment system in which OA has been set up will undoubtedly face various problems. Counter measures like re-education, re-hiring of middle-aged laborers so that they can be useful in the new system, and also the new dimension of OA in regard to health disorders, etc., must be taken into consideration to avoid and/or resolve what could become major problems. Here, it is clear that the new dimension in personnel management along with human resource development will come into play.

The studies cited above, together with the Economic White Paper and the Manpower Survey by the Prime Minister's Office lead us to suspect that the problems caused by the new tendency towards increased use of OA and ME in Japan may not only bring about environmental change for personnel management, but also unfavourable changes in society as well. Needless to say, even through a large part of public opinion seems to believe that technological innovation will not decrease the overall level of employment, workers should be directed into new fields, so that the demand in certain areas is met by a sufficient supply of labor.

The demand-supply relation for qualified labor will change to some extent under the influence of new technologies of both the OA and ME type. Specifically, the demand for labor will be clearly polarized into highly skilled and very simple types. Labor policy to develop human ability correspondingly from a new view-point will become more imortant. Up to today, technological innovation has been understood rather more as a factor to improve the quality of capital equipment, but it will become more relevant to labor in the near future, and its impacts on personnel management should be considered with greater emphasis on management theory, so that solutions for better allocation of labor will be provided in time.

Appendix: Summary of Office Automation Reference Survey

(1) Active Zone for OA

    a: Industry Group

Machinery and Electrical	22.7 %
Food and Chemicals	18.1
Telephone and Transportation	17.0

    b: Amount of Capital

less 500 million yen	30.4
1 --- 3 billion yen	20.4
5 --- 10 billion yen	11.9

    c: Number of Employees

500 --- 1000	20.3
2000 --- 5000	18.9
5000 over	17.8

(2) Active Need for OA

Productivity on Office Management	37.8
Mechnization of Simple Operations	34.4
Personnel Speed and Reliability	29.3
Information Processing	17.4
OA Mood	2.6

(3) Performance and Moral Rate

	Company Rate (%)	Performance Rate (index)	Employee Moral Rate (index)
Active towards Computer	46.2	5074	3486
Indifferent to Computer	37.0	4999	3340
Passive towards Computer	16.8	4843	3236

(4) Active Area for OA in Office Management

	On Controlling	On Planning
Data Processing	50.4 %	22.2 %
Finance and Accounting	48.1	35.6
Sales	39.6	35.6
Personnel	35.6	31.9
General	29.3	35.9

(5) OA Instrument

    a: Currently

Facsimile	54.8 %
Personnel Computer	48.5
Japanese Word Processor	40.0
On-line Terminal	35.9
Office Computer	31.5

    b: Near Future

Japanese Word Processor	54.8
Personnel Computer	46.3
On-line Terminal	39.6
Office Computer	33.3
Facsimile	28.5

    c: IC Years Planning

Voice Input	37.8
Large Electronic File	27.0
Laser Beam Communication	22.2
Electronic Mail	18.9
Electronic Congress System	18.5

Impacts of Microelectronics
on Human Resource Development in Production Systems
- an Empirical Research of Factory Automation in Japan -

Kazumasa Takemori

1 Tendency of Productivity in Manufacturing Companies

In recent years there has been a marked increase in
Japan's productivity. This is largely due to the investment in new plants and machines which produce a higher
level of productivity. Most of these machines are e-
quipped with microelectronics for higher performance. As
a typical example of the introduction of microelectronics, industrial robots have contributed to the replacement of workshops where only skilled workers were used.
Now the process at the workshops is more easily operated
by fewer unskilled workers and productivity is higher
than before. In turn, many unpleasant and health-risk
jobs have been eliminated, benefiting workers. It is
evident that the technological and managerial evolution
will be significant in forecasting the future development
of productivity.

At this point we examine Chart I and Table I which give
information about recent tendency of productivity in
Japan. Chart I shows productivity in a two-dimensional
comparison between 1979 and 1980. In these two years it
was characteristic that manufacturing processes were
reviewed in order to identify advantages and disadvantages in all companies, and that each company then strove
to increase efficiency. Most of companies realized their
high productivity by investing in new plants, defining
their goals as:

a) to effectively redesign their machines and form
   unified production systems out of the complexity of
   new and old machinery,

b) to change processes from manual operation to automation, and

c) to reduce the number of employees.

We exclude petroleum related companies, ranked from 1 to
7, and natural resources importers, numbered 8 and 9,
from our examination. Their higher added values are due
to the yen-dollar currency fluctuation, not because of
their technological or management factors.

Observing the comparison between 1979 and 1980, we
recognize that productivity in Japan is steadily soaring
upward. The 1979 rankings have an index range of 50 -
160, while in 1980 the index ranges from 130 - 490. With
the exception of a few extraordinary cases, most
companies faced difficulties in attaining higher productivity as they developed and applied technological
innovations and improvements. Thus it is important that
they added human resource development to their efforts.

According to Table I, we observe this general tendency of
Japanese productivity:

Increases continued until 1973. Chemical and iron related
industries attained high rates, e.g., paper, ammonite,
iron rolling, steel casting, and electric wires. However,
a drastic decrease took place in 1974 and 1975. The
previously mentioned industries were greatly influenced
by the 1973 Oil-Crisis. After 1976, growth rates were low
but stable. Since that time industrial structure has
changed regarding chemical and iron industries. Pulp,
soda, and car show stable excellence.

Furthermore, the Statistics and Information Department of
the Ministry of Labor, analyzes the tendency of productivity in relation to other elements, such as; change in
output, input of labor, and allocated personnels. As for
the latter, it states; (The Monthly Labor statistics and

Chart I

Productivity 1979/1980

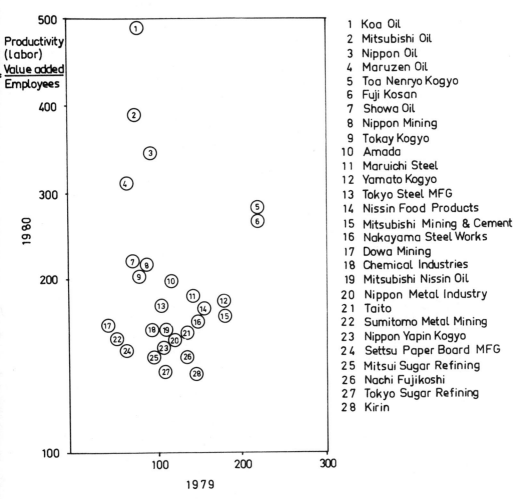

1 Koa Oil
2 Mitsubishi Oil
3 Nippon Oil
4 Maruzen Oil
5 Toa Nenryo Kogyo
6 Fuji Kosan
7 Showa Oil
8 Nippon Mining
9 Tokay Kogyo
10 Amada
11 Maruichi Steel
12 Yamato Kogyo
13 Tokyo Steel MFG
14 Nissin Food Products
15 Mitsubishi Mining & Cement
16 Nakayama Steel Works
17 Dowa Mining
18 Chemical Industries
19 Mitsubishi Nissin Oil
20 Nippon Metal Industry
21 Taito
22 Sumitomo Metal Mining
23 Nippon Yapin Kogyo
24 Settsu Paper Board MFG
25 Mitsui Sugar Refining
26 Nachi Fujikoshi
27 Tokyo Sugar Refining
28 Kirin

Source: original data from the Nikkei Sangyo Shimbun, Sept 1, 1980, Tokyo, Japan

Notice: encircled numbers show rankings in 1980

Design: Takemori
Graphicdesign: IFEP Freiburg i.Br. Kö 87.2

Table I GROWTH RATE OF PRODUCTIVITY BY INDUSTRIES

classification	1971	'72	'73	'74	'75	'76	'77	'78	'79	'80	'81	'82
all industries	3.8	8.6	12.2	-5.1	1.5	12.4	0.6	8.2	8.4 (8.1)	0.9	-2.0	-0.9
cotton spinning	4.1	9.5	5.3	-2.0	-1.5	14.3	-0.4	10.4	19.5	-3.1	-2.2	7.6
wool spinning	4.8	12.2	7.0	-11.0	13.6	12.1	5.5	3.0	6.5	2.4	4.3	-0.7
rayon cloths	9.2	4.4	9.4	-4.7	6.9	10.5	7.7	9.1	3.0	6.3	-1.2	2.3
veneer, board	8.7	12.6	8.8	-3.8	11.3	2.3	4.4	13.6	9.6	-2.3	1.7	4.3
pulp	11.6	12.0	10.1	-9.8	-1.8	10.7	5.9	2.8	10.4	-3.1	4.6	5.0
paper	3.6	4.9	22.3	-17.9	10.1	11.3	7.5	6.3	7.0	0.3	6.9	2.3
ammonite	23.8	22.0	1.4	-3.8	4.6	-34.2	38.6	9.1	15.1	-30.5	-2.6	3.3
soda	11.0	12.6	3.4	-10.8	0.6	-5.1	12.0	3.8	27.8	0.5	2.5	8.6
rayon	11.4	18.1	10.3	-19.1	17.6	17.5	10.2	9.3	4.6	1.7	5.3	2.6
tire tubes	4.7	11.6	12.6	-1.6	2.5	11.1	4.0	10.1	12.6	4.9	0.0	2.5
cement	2.4	14.0	12.3	-6.6	4.2	20.7	12.9	6.8	5.3	0.8	-3.0	-4.6
iron refining	0.7	7.4	13.2	-7.8	-4.3	13.1	-10.2	5.9	9.1	3.7	-3.3	-5.6
iron rolling	-3.7	6.3	19.1	-7.1	-5.6	19.8	-18.3	6.7	5.3	-10.9	-5.7	-2.3
steel casting	-3.6	7.9	16.1	1.6	-3.4	10.3	6.8	7.3	10.5	3.6	1.3	0.6
electric wires	8.2	14.1	15.4	-35.2	20.1	13.0	12.2	16.2	3.0	7.4	4.2	-4.1
lathe	-12.1	-0.1	13.5	-8.5	-40.4	27.6	13.8	4.3	6.3	7.0	-15.4	-18.1
bearings	2.6	18.2	10.7	9.1	-21.5	19.4	9.2	13.0	7.2	18.8	2.2	2.5
electric motors	7.6	11.2	7.7	-2.6	2.8	8.2	10.8	7.0	11.4	5.6	9.0	7.6
cars	12.2	6.5	4.0	1.2	8.6	8.4	3.3	9.6	5.9	8.9	-6.7	-2.2
watchs	0.6	16.9	0.4	8.8	-4.3	15.1	10.8	13.0	11.1	-	-	-

Source: The Monthly Labor Statistics and Research Bulletin, Vol. 35, No. 12, December 1983, p. 31

Note: Data are for the months October and November. = decrease

Research Bulletin, December 1983)

... Reasons for the decrease in all levels of industry and in other cases where a decrease in number of employees has been observed, are: (1) a demand decrease of 54.8 %, (2) efficiency up 38.6 % by means of process control and work study, (3) mechanization up 33.1 %, (4) education and training up 23.7 %.

2 Background and Development of Automated Production Systems

In the 1960s Japanese industries began to expand their international trade. In order to produce better products they learned new management methods: QC, IE, or VA. They introduced and developed automated production lines. They sought to increase efficiency of total plants by rapidly replacing their manually operated machinery with semi-automated, and then semi-automated with fully-automated. Today Japanese industries are working at a more advanced level of FA. Table II shows large-scale investment from the latter half of the 1960s to 1973, then descending from 1974, and gradually increasing from 1978 to today.

We recognize from this table that structural change also occures in the Japanese economy. Table II gives the following sequence of events; the Nixon Shock in 1971, the Oil-Crisis of 1973 which demaged the Japanese economy, the surprisingly high deficits in NET INCOME BEFORE TAXES for the four years since 1974 and, after 1978 the return of the NET INCOME BEFORE TAXES to their previous high level. At this point, though, the LONG-TERM DEBTS show a gradual decrease due to companies' efforts to attain a non-debt financial policy, and LABOR COSTS show little increase.

Statistical data on the top ten electric companies make it clear that the tendency of the turnover rate of

Table II   INVESTMENT AND RELATED STATISTICS OF JAPANESE MANUFACTURING COMPANIES

YEAR	1966	1967	1968	1969	1970	1971	1972	1973
INVESTMENT	16.4	2.5	4.6	10.1	-0.5	-6.1	3.8	14.0
LONG TERM DEBT	0.6	4.9	4.5	4.8	5.9	4.0	0.6	1.4
NET-INCOME BEFORE TAX	19.6	9.5	9.3	13.1	-7.2	-7.7	28.7	12.2
LABOR COST	5.1	8.4	9.1	10.5	9.0	5.2	7.6	14.5

	1974	1975	1976	1977	1978	1979	1980	1981
=	-4.7	-3.1	8.3	-9.8	3.6	-2.1	6.2	7.1
=	4.6	4.0	1.9	0.5	2.4	1.3	0.8	0.8
=	-33.4	-65.6	-38.3	-4.9	17.5	23.1	-8.3	16.8
=	10.1	1.7	4.1	2.6	1.7	3.5	3.8	3.7

Source: Statistical Bureau, the Bank of Japan, SHORT TERM ECONOMIC OBSERVATORY ANNUAL OF MAIN COM-
   PANIES IN JAPAN,

Note: 1. figures are prozential, showing the increased rate compared to the proceding year

   2. INVESTMENT and LONG-TERM DEBT are for the October-December quarter

   3. NET INCOME BEFORE TAX and LABOR CCST are an average of first six months and the rest
      of the year.

Table III   TURNOVER RATE OF TANGIBLE FIXED ASSETS (top five)

(times/year)

Company	43 (1968)	48 (1973)	49 (1974)	50 (1975)	51 (1976)	52 (1977)	53 (1978)
Matsushita Electric	10.67	13.26	13.30	11.52	16.69	19.09	20.71
Hitachi Manufacturing	4.98	5.88	6.44	6.54	7.37	7.37	7.53
Toshiba	4.50	5.12	5.74	6.01	6.04	6.40	7.18
Mitsubishi Electric	5.42	5.54	5.42	5.32	6.22	6.91	7.35
Nippon Electric	4.29	5.18	5.11	5.72	6.39	6.65	6.64

Source: Kyoikusha, ED, BUSINESS COMPARISON OF ELECTRIC INDUSTRIES, 1980

tangible fixed assets has improved greatly since 1974. There are two reasons. One is the global semi-conductor boom since 1977, and the second is the more effective use of investments.

In the ten year period investment practically doubled;

	Million Yen		
	1968		1978
Matsushita Electric	43,768	---	77,153
Hitachi Manufact.	109,090	---	200,527
Toshiba	96,316	---	172,608
Mitsubishi Electric	52,846	---	127,110
Nippon Electric	34,852	---	92,730

These companies consider the use of microelectronics and FA as one reason for their success. This is symbolic for the future development of FA. A report published by the Japan Research Total Institute analyzes these tendencies:

a) ME revolution related industries forecast their demands using a high, increasing rate.

b) A high rate of growth is expected in many fields, such as: new raw materials, FA machines, biotechnology, medicine and health, computer application, electronics and semi-conductor, and OA instruments.

c) Chart II shows areas where managements plan to increase investement for next five years.

d) Office Automation (OA) and FA are ranked highly in business strategy. As for the present status of FA introduction, 18.3 % of all industries introduced NC robots, 15.4 % unvariable sequence robots, 11.6 % variable sequence robots, 10.3 % playback robots, 3.3 % intelligent robots, and 11.9 % manual manipulators.
A similiar tendency as above can be seen in the transportation machinery industry and electrical machinery industry. See Chart III.

Chart II

Goals and Fields of Investments/
Next five years

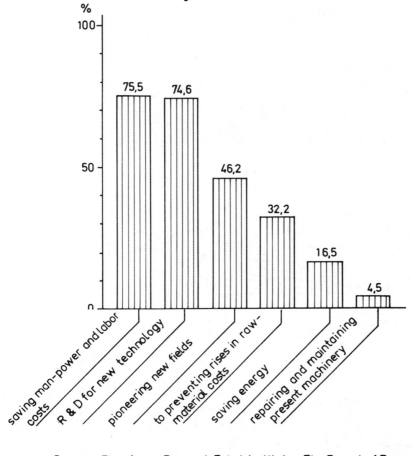

Source: The Japan Research Total Institute, The Report of Research
on Changing Index of Industry and Society, 1983, p. 22

Design: Takemori
Graphicdesign: IFEP Freiburg i.Br. | Kö 87.2

Chart III

Present Introduction of FA Machines

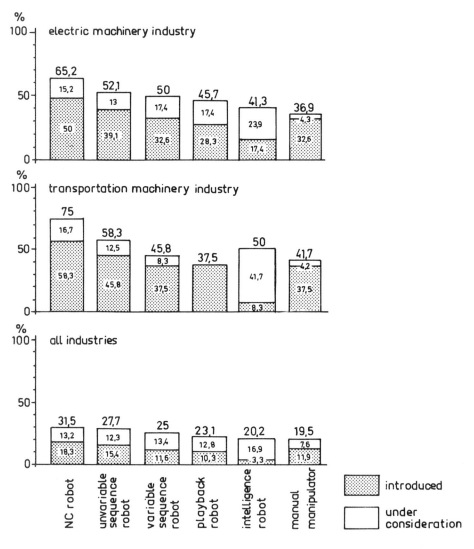

Source: The Japan Research Total Institute, ibid., p.24

Design: Takemori
Graphicdesign: IFEP Freiburg i.Br. Kö 87.2

At this point we must also recognize the opinions of the labor union. The growing investment in such modern machines requires a new relationship between workers and management. It is obvious that the labor union has conceded to the companies' basic strategy of introducing rationalized investments, because they agreed to producing more high-technology-intensive and highly value-added products. In 1982, however, the labor union for the Electric Industry (DENROREN) declared the following principles for microelectronics production systems.

a) Before introducing microelectronic machinery, complete coordination should be established and an agreement with the labor union should be confirmed. Otherwise the introduction will not be accepted.

b) The introduction can never be disadvantageous to employment and labor conditions. In cases where introduction would have a direct influence on employment (i.e. dismissal) the plan for F.A. would never be considered.

c) Sufficient consideration should be given by the company concerning safety measures. After the introduction of microelectronic machinery, the labor union will monitor workshops to insure that the measures are enforced.

DENROREN also established detail items and guidelines for the problems of microelectronics introduction.

Labor Unions do not see the serious disadvantages of the microelectronics revolution now, but nor do they see its future as optimistic. This problem will occur as structural changes in the generation hierarchy continue to be made. Soon the majority of the Japanese population will consist of middle-aged and old men. For this reason various preparatory steps must be taken in this rapid advancing microelectronics revolution.

3 Elements of Feasibility Study for the Introduction Microelectronics (ME) Supported Systems

In general, a feasibility study is analyzed by calculating input and output. Input is the revenue, profit, or cost-down, and output is purchased costs, leasing costs, capital costs, or R&D costs. We have several kinds of feasibility studies for investment decisions:

a) the capital non-considered method ... 1. costs comparing method, 2. capital collection period method

b) the considered method ... 1. return of investment method, 2. profit index method

c) the time non-considered method ... the estimation of methods a) and b) without the time consideration

d) and the time considered method ... the estimation of methods a) and b) with time consideration

In every case, we will be able to correct the figures for output, because output can be easily calculated with amounts expended or accrued. Input, however, is more difficult to determine because revenue or profit is uncertain. These methods are introduced in a middle or long-term business plan.

When introducing microelectronic machines and FA machines, many other elements besides those mentioned should be included in estimation. Microelectronics and FA have many advantages over the traditional high performance machines, e.g., materials and inventories work-in-process diminished, lead time shortened, labor costs diminished, coordination of output volume facilitated, and a high reliability of quality control automated. Shigeru Kobayashi emphasizes a new "investment effectiveness study" with new management philosophy. Former studies are based upon the MAPI method of 1949 and the new MAPI method of 1958, and include various methods.

Chart IV

Estimated Years of Investment Collection of FA -Machinery

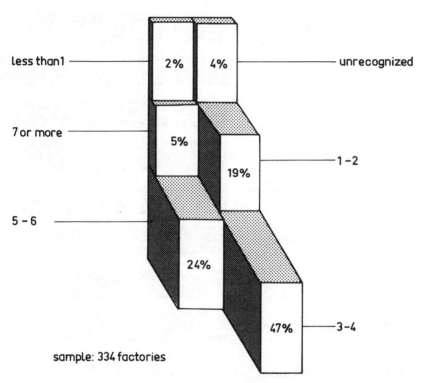

less than1 ——————————— 2% 4% ——————————— unrecognized

7 or more ——————————— 5%

                                    19% ——————————— 1-2

5 - 6 ———————————

                   24%

                              47% ——————— 3-4

sample: 334 factories

Source: Nikkei Mechanical, ED, A Guidebook to Mechatronics Japan '84, The
        Nihon Keizai Shimbun, 1984, p.71

| Design: Takemori |
| Graphicdesign: IFEP Freiburg i.Br. | Kö 87.2 |

Chart V

Satisfaction Degree after FA Introduction

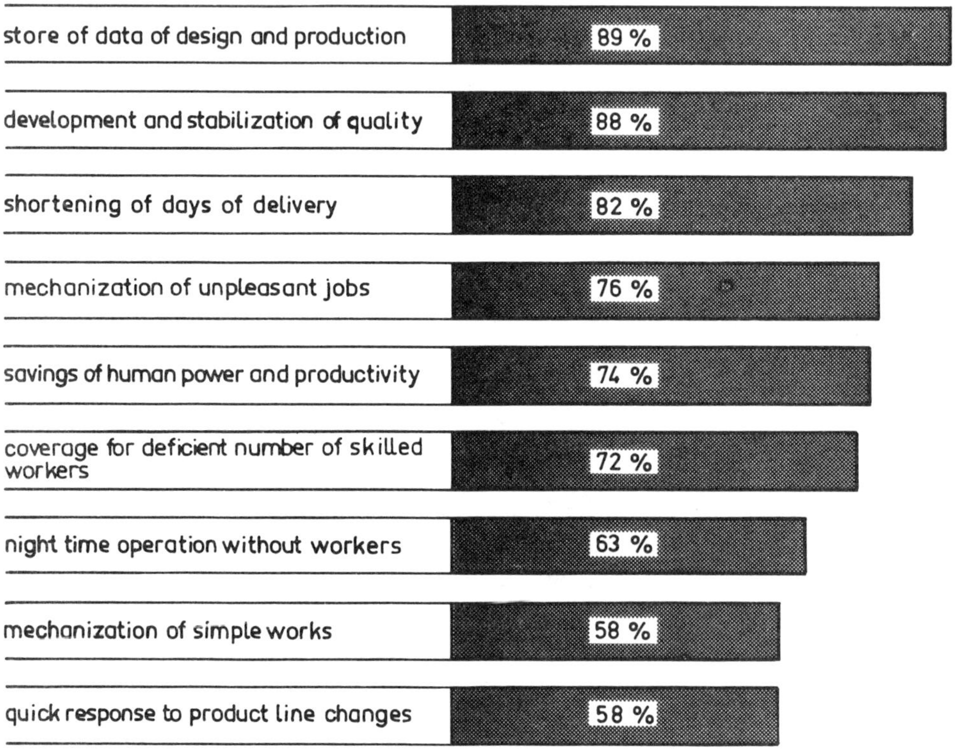

store of data of design and production	89 %
development and stabilization of quality	88 %
shortening of days of delivery	82 %
mechanization of unpleasant jobs	76 %
savings of human power and productivity	74 %
coverage for deficient number of skilled workers	72 %
night time operation without workers	63 %
mechanization of simple works	58 %
quick response to product line changes	58 %

Source : Nikkei Mechanical, ED, ibid., p.72

Design : Takemori	
Graphicdesign : IFEP Freiburg i.Br	Kö 87.2

While these traditional methods are all based upon investment in machinery, or tools operated by man power, this new method defines investment as being based upon microelectronics.

In one Japanese company, the average investment amount in FA is estimated to be around one billion yen. Unfortunately there is no data showing the number of companies who utilize a feasibility study before investing. According to research, a period of three or four years is necessary to collect such data. The figures that are available are smaller in comparison with investment in new machinery. Another point to consider is that small-sized factories never estimate the length of time that collection of capital takes them.

In a sample of 364 factories, 99 % agreed on the effectiveness of FA introduction. According to the sample, the factories ranked their goals before introduction as follows:

1) to save human power and to increase productivity

2) to develop and stabilize the quality of products

3) to replace simple works of men with mechanization

However, the satisfaction degrees (effectiveness/goal) shows different rankings from the above three goals:

1) that they could store data for design and production

2) that they could develop and stabilize product quality

3) that they could shorten the number of delivery days

It is interesting that the top ranked goal "to save human power and to increase productivity" is only ranked fifth after FA introduction. The third goal, of replacing manual work with mechanization, was ranked eighth after FA introduction. The satisfaction degrees are shown in Chart V.

It is to expect, that the lower ranked items will be the targets of future developments in the field of FA.

4 Education Systems and Their Effects on ME Innovated Industries

New production systems developed along with the large-scale introduction of FA or microelectronic machines. Serious problems for the workers have also developed. In 1983, the Employment Promotion Project Organization polled technical workers concerning technological innovation. They found that the workers evaluate "innovation" as the following: the reduction of overly strenuous and dirty jobs, the improvement of productivity through stabilization of product quality, and as the reduction of manpower in operation. The technical workers also expressed their uneasiness about their employment, workshop changes, obsolescence of their technique, and mental fatigue (see Chart VI).

In other research by the former Japan Total Research Institute, the same tendency of uneasiness was found in the company as well. This report researched the influences of the introduction of OA or FA machinery, or instruments, and evaluating the uneasiness or anxiety. As can be seen in Chart VII, the majority of the responses were "unanxious/not uneasy". Anxiety, however was expressed for the "cost of purchase and maintenance" and "trouble in production departments or office treatment in case of disorder". Companies are most anxious about initial costs on introduction of instruments, their running costs, the chaos of operation in case of unexpected disorder, and replacement of men. These results do not concur with the general opinion that not only chaos and disapplicability against OA/FA introduction occurs, but that office and factory environments change, and difficulties in re-allocating men arise.

Chart VI

Technical Worker's Response on technological Innovation

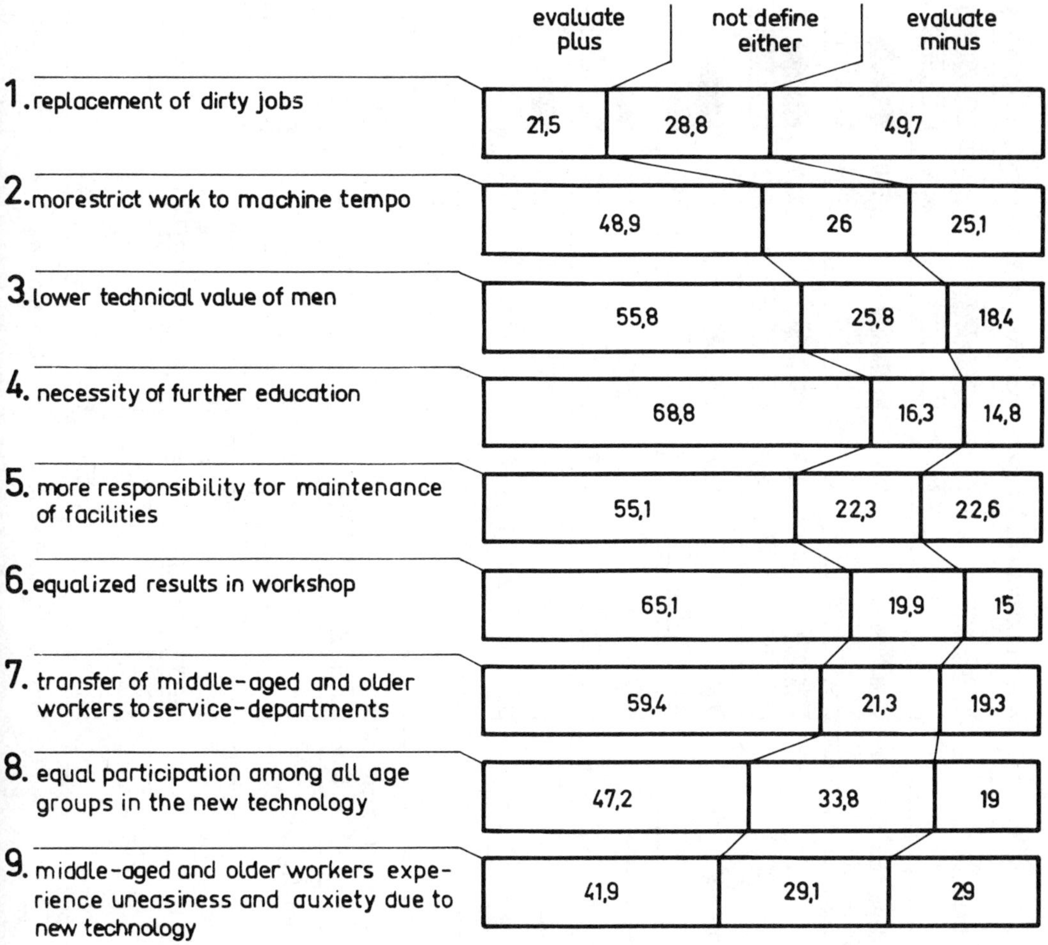

	evaluate plus	not define either	evaluate minus
1. replacement of dirty jobs	21,5	28,8	49,7
2. more strict work to machine tempo	48,9	26	25,1
3. lower technical value of men	55,8	25,8	18,4
4. necessity of further education	68,8	16,3	14,8
5. more responsibility for maintenance of facilities	55,1	22,3	22,6
6. equalized results in workshop	65,1	19,9	15
7. transfer of middle-aged and older workers to service-departments	59,4	21,3	19,3
8. equal participation among all age groups in the new technology	47,2	33,8	19
9. middle-aged and older workers experience uneasiness and auxiety due to new technology	41,9	29,1	29

Source: Employment Promotion Project Organization, ED, Human Resources Development in the Era of Mechatronics, Printing Bureau of the Ministry of Finance, 1983, p.85

Design: Takemori	
Graphicdesign: IFEP Freiburg i.Br.	Kö 87.2

Chart VII Influences by introduction of OA/FA

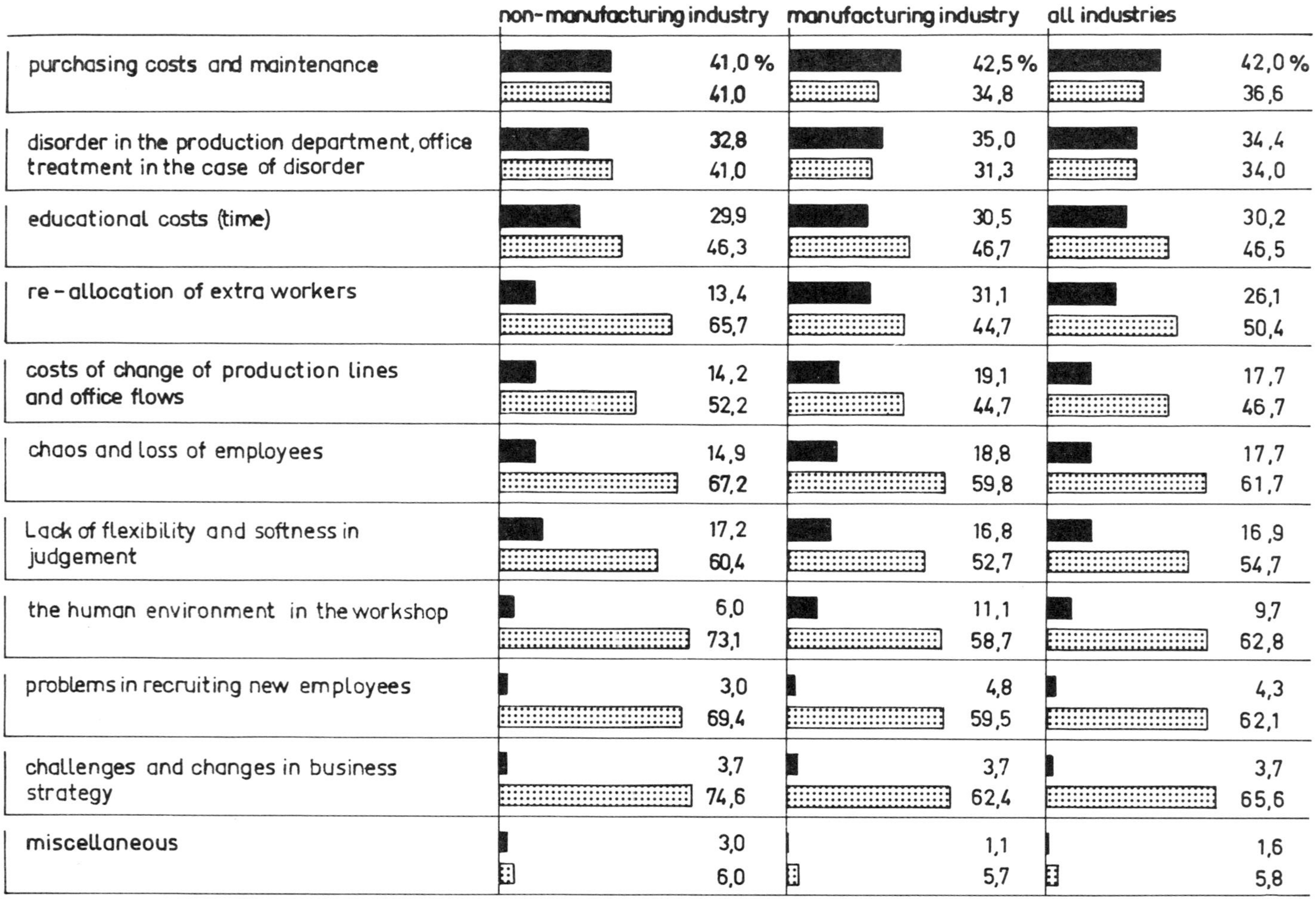

	non-manufacturing industry		manufacturing industry		all industries	
	uneasy, anxious	uneasy, unanxious	uneasy, anxious	uneasy, unanxious	uneasy, anxious	uneasy, unanxious
purchasing costs and maintenance	41,0 %	41,0	42,5 %	34,8	42,0 %	36,6
disorder in the production department, office treatment in the case of disorder	32,8	41,0	35,0	31,3	34,4	34,0
educational costs (time)	29,9	46,3	30,5	46,7	30,2	46,5
re-allocation of extra workers	13,4	65,7	31,1	44,7	26,1	50,4
costs of change of production lines and office flows	14,2	52,2	19,1	44,7	17,7	46,7
chaos and loss of employees	14,9	67,2	18,8	59,8	17,7	61,7
Lack of flexibility and softness in judgement	17,2	60,4	16,8	52,7	16,9	54,7
the human environment in the workshop	6,0	73,1	11,1	58,7	9,7	62,8
problems in recruiting new employees	3,0	69,4	4,8	59,5	4,3	62,1
challenges and changes in business strategy	3,7	74,6	3,7	62,4	3,7	65,6
miscellaneous	3,0	6,0	1,1	5,7	1,6	5,8

■ uneasy, anxious
▨ uneasy, unanxious

Source: Japan Research Total Institute, op. cit., p. 26

Design: Takemori
Graphicdesign: IFEP Freiburg i. Br. Kö 872

In view of the two research studies' results, we see the immense importance of education. Education programs may vary from one company to another, but one common denominator is clear, namely the upgraded abilities of human resources. If managed properly, education will solve most problems related to the new technological innovations. Whereas efforts to educate workers in the 20 - 40 age group have been met with success, efforts to educate the middle-aged and older workers have been stymied. These groups lack flexibility and adaptability needed for the more sophisticated knowledge requirements related to FA and microelectronics. A Ministry of Labor report warns that these workers must first complete the proper technical courses before being placed in their workshop jobs. The expansion of occupational areas for older men is also recommended. The report also emphasizes the importance of education programs for the improvement of human resources, including: life-time education, new official job training by local governments, and the establishment of an official qualification examination for technique development.

According to the 1983 research report by the Ministry of Labor, education and FA are stated as follows:

a) 60.0 % of factories had education programs for workers who remain in the same workshops after ME introduction. Larger-scaled operations reported a higher rate. But even in factories with less than 299 workers, the rate was 57.5 %

b) Among factories in a) 76.7 % used education and training programs held by either manufacturers or retailers. 53.5 % had intra-company education and training. The larger-scaled factories had a higher percentage of intra-company education programs.

c) Among factories without education or training programs, 51.5 % answered that necessary techniques were obtained through OJT. And 39.1 % answered that they did not need education. A high percentage of large-scaled factories answered that necessary techniques were obtained through OJT. Factories with less than 299 workers answered almost in same percentage as OJT and education unnecessary.

This research reveals that Japanese companies make very good use of OJT. This type of training may be useful in combination with motivation and participation, that is to say, small group activities and QC circles.

5 Case Studies on Manufacturing Firms

5.1 Case of Ebara Manufacturing Company

Ebara Manufacturing Company is famous for its effective education systems and its FA practice. Its data for the 1983 accounting period is as follows:

a) capital   10,513 million Yen
b) annual sales   151,600 million Yen
c) employees   4,600
d) Product lines   hydro-machine, boiler, turbin, oil-pressure instrument, air-conditioning machine, anti-pollution engineering, atomic instrument

Its basic education philosophy is that the Ebara of tomorrow fully depends upon today's education, which is organized to fit the ability level, and aptitude of each employee. In addition, its education systems primarily target the development of fully creative men.

The nature of the Ebara education systems and their curriculum is to support self-development studies, where employees use their free time for the purpose of increasing their work level and developing their personalities. The systems have two levels of goals:

1) to make men creatively active for the company's needs, and

2) to make all men indispensable to the company and sensitive to social needs.

Chart VIII shows the educational systems chart.
To some extent, Ebara has developed perfect automation lines without direct workers. Its education programs for workshop transfer and re-allocated workers have been developed through three major steps. The first step, in 1974 was an education program primarily on sales techniques in order to transfer workers from plants to retail and maintenance service departments. 70 young men were selected and received the education. In 1976, a second step entailed the education of 30 young men for a transfer to the designing and engineering departments. The third step was a program in 1982 to prepare workers for jobs in designing departements. 40 young men were selected and are presently being educated.

There are many other education courses for workshop transfer. They are at an equal level with curriculum offered in colleges. Around two hundred men completed their courses and were easily transfered to new work-shops. Essential to a smooth transfer is the new super-visor or manager's relationship to the new worker. In fact, nurturing the human relationships is an important task of all management. The key to motivating the new man, then, lies in elevating his self esteem by communicating the necessity of his experience and expertise for the workshop.

According to its data, Ebara shows a 70 % satisfaction rate for transfered employees. Other correlations between education and transfers are not available at this time.

Chart VIII

Systems Chart of Education in a Company

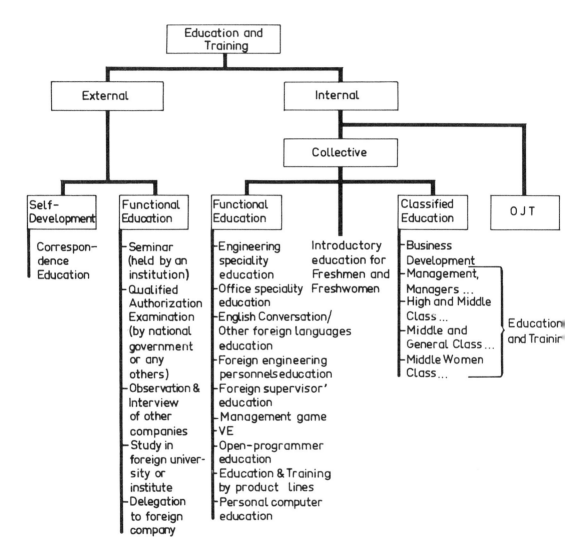

Source: Shigeru Shimizu, "Education of company in changing period-
Learn the case," Diamond Recruite Information, Vol. 9, No. 6.
July/August, 1983, pp. 42–46; with permission of author.

Design: Takemori
Graphicdesign: IFEP Freiburg i. Br. Kö 87.2

5.2 Case of Nachi-Fujikoshi Company

Nachi-Fujikoshi Company is a leading bearings manufacturer, who has recently become famous for ist robots. Its
data for the 1982 accounting period is as follows:

a) capital   9,567 million Yen
b) annual sales   64,624 million Yen
c) employees   5,200 million Yen

Nachi-Fujikoshi has sought to develop its human resources. Managers encourage workers to pass any kind of
technique skill examination. 50 % of school fees or costs
for correspondence education are reimbursed after successful completion. Nachi emphasizes OJT and proposal
systems by QC circles. It is mandatory that each worker
submit at least four ideas every month. Excellent proposals are honored with prizes in either category A, B,
C, or D. A, B, and C prize winners are given prize money
while D winners receive soap. This rule applies to all
employees under the foreman (kakaricho). QC circles are
held after duty. Such movements are primarily arbitrary,
but they are now in real systems. It may prove difficult
to hold these after duty.

On inspection of the Nachi workshops, we are surprised to
find their machines and tools in perfect working order,
and appear brand new. This is the result of Nachis TQC
and TPM (total production maintenance program). On
foundation memorialday in 1982, Nachi started a clean-up
action for its 5,000 machines. Soon results began to
appear in several areas: small malfunctions were found
before operation; labor accidents decreased remarkably;
attitudes on duty improved; clearing time shortened from
ten to two minutes. Also, all machines are now painted
grey, instead of green or brown, in order to easily
detect dust and defects.

Another important area for education at Nachi-Fujikoshi

is the middle management. These employees are educated by engineers about the most recent technological developments. This targets development of managements to deepen knowledge of mechatronization. Such education programs are now useful in developing engineers and R&D staffs.

Nachi, as all other companies, also has educational problems. The present retirementage in the company is 59, but every two years it is raised a year. Soon the majority of employees will be middle-aged and older. Although difficulties due to this pattern are not yet explicit, survival in the ever rapidly changing ME innovation will depend on the successful reorganization of the education systems.

6 New Education Systems by Various Sectors - a Proposal

Companies have endeavored to match ME innovation using education. This education, for the most part, has been composed by OJT, seminars, correspondence education, and employees' independent self-development.

Total development of human resources cannot be achieved by the company alone. Various sectors will have to cooperate to bring about total development of workers abilities. These sectors are: university, industry, and local and national government.

What type of men will be targeted in ME innovation? In his research report entitled, "What attributes are expected among men in business in 1980s?", Nikkeiren found the following results among machinery and manufacturer companies:

a) 1. active, 2. ability to predict future (companies with less than 500 men)

b) 1. vital, 2. unwillingly ideal 3. coordinative (companies with less than 1,000 men)

c) 1. leadership, 2. creative and ambitious (companies with less than 500 men)

d) 1. highly professional, 2. coordinative between other departments 3. ability to expand business opportunity and develop new products (companies with more than 5,001 men)

e) 1. intellectual and talented, 2. leadership, 3. ambitious, advancive and active (companies with less than 3,000 men)

f) 1. possesses a wealth of business knowledge, 2. decisive with good judgement, 3. creative (companies with less than 3,000 men)

These attributes are then seen as the goal of all education. And creating an environment where men will develop such attributes is the major task for education systems. If industries continue their present educational course, desired results will not be attained. In interviews with several companies Hiroaki Wakuta (1981) found that business needs are too dogmatic to pursue long-term profit and that educational staffs tend to judge applicability according to it's ability to yield quick profit. He concluded, that new programs should be created to provide for the education of new relationships between employees and corporate organizations.

An education complex should be created from the combination of industrial, university, and governmental resources. The proposed complex would provide for human resource development through:

a) a communication salon

b) holding study meetings and seminars

c) cooperative research

d) collecting, storing and processing information

e) developing business opportunities

By these means, the education complex would have the
necessary basis to respond to changing and varying
business needs with proper planning, production and
marketing. Big business are not far from such a basis,
while medium or small business lack several factors.
Especially in regions distant from Tokyo and Osaka, such
a proposed education complex would be readily received.
For instance, Nagoya City has started planning its
Industrial Research Institute and a re-education center.
The projected center will be managed by teachers from
business, by academic and public institutes of research
or examination, if necessary from other nations, by a
committee composed of representatives delegated from
business, academic, municipal or national government, and
to have a training in a common experimental factory with
sufficient machinery and tools.

Takenori Saito (1981) suggests these three types of
university-industry cooperation:

1) donations by the industry to the university or its
   scholarship foundation

2) the development and preparation of a cooperative
   curriculum implemented through: the exchange of
   teaching staffs, education of industry personnels in
   university courses, participation of university faculties in industrial education, and work training for
   university students in industry

3) cooperative conferences, study meetings, or common
   research and development projects, as well as research
   and consultation to industry

Saito notes that present interaction between the two
sectors is minimal. He agrees with research by Nikkeiren,
in that much progress would be made if companies would
invite university faculties to intracompany education,
and would encourage personnel to participate in study
meetings or community courses held by the university. The

tendency, however, is that such contact between industry and university fails to develop into a continuous interaction. This negative tendency is further compounded by industry's priority emphasis on OJT and collective education. In Nikkeiren's research, companies ranked job rotation and self-developmentassistance much lower, with education gained in outside institutions following to the bottom of their list.

Saito concludes that university education is seldom used by industry, and that the quality of education in universities is not considered very high in Japan.

Nevertheless, a total education complex is necessary for the total development of human resources. At this point, the plan of Ministry of International Trade and Industry (MITI) the national goverment, must be examined.

MITI is promoting a policy to develop greater potential in overall regional technology. This policy is an exten- tion of its Third National Plan for All-Inclusive Devel- opment in which it had set with an emphasis on regions. There are, however, limits in the economy, energy and resources, growing and economic competition from under- developed nations. MITI is setting policies to solve critical problems and to bring about a new evolution by:

a) strengthening capabilities for development of techno- logy for regional industry

b) extending the regional function into high-technology and top-level technological industry, and into re- search and development

c) utilizing natural resources and human resources in regional society

d) developing various social systems

e) and establishing a cooperative complex among industry, university and the local and national government as well as promoting business communications between different fields.

These regional promotion policies have been in effect since 1982. In items d) and e) we observe the strategy "techno-polis", which targets the establishment of coordination between industry (high technology industry group), research (university school of engineers and civilian research institute), and the environment life (comfortable living conditions with natural and architectural coordination). "Techno-polis" circulates power into the regional top-level technological industry, enables the companies to develop products with a higher added value. These policies are not simply industrial introduction to regional areas, but allow for the establishment of a complex including the industrial zone, academic zone, and habital zone. Within this complex, university and research institutes bring forth human resources with high abilities. The interactive function of techno-polis is shown as the Chart IX.

Gratitude

I express my hearty gratitude to professor mitsuo kamiya, my research conductor, and to Mr. Masao Tezuka, Vice-President and Executive Director od Nachi-Fuijkoshi for my case study research.

Chart IX

Interactive Function of Techno-Polis

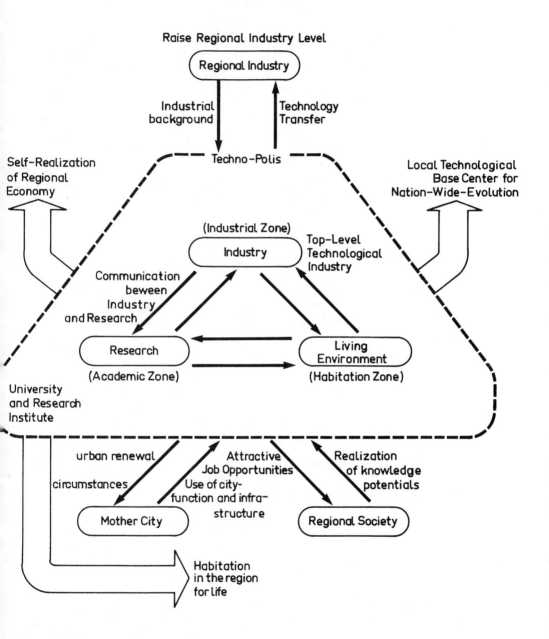

Source: Watanabe, S. ED, The Era of Regional Technology, Tsusho-sangyo-chosa-kai, 1982, p. 260

References

I. Publications of Government or Institutes

LABOR UNION OF ELECTRIC INDUSTRIES: Microelectronics Innovation and Industrial Policy; The sixth agenda for the 30th union convention, 1982, Tokyo, Japan.

THE FIFTH EMPLOYMENT COUNCIL FOR THE MINISTER OF LABOR: Perspective of Employment until 1990 and the Direction of the Employment Policy, 1983, Tokyo, Japan.

STATISTICS AND INFORMATION DEPARTMENT OF THE MINISTRY OF LABOR: Summary of Research on Technological Innovation and Labor, 1983, Tokyo, Japan.

EMPLOYMENT PROMOTION PROJECT ORGANIZATION, (Ed.): Human Resource Development in the Era of Mechatronics, Printing Bureau of the Ministry of Finance, 1983, Tokyo, Japan.

JAPAN TOTAL RESEARCH INSTITUTE: The Research Report on the Changing Index of Industry and Society, 1983, Tokyo, Japan.

STATISTICAL BUREAU OF THE BANK OF JAPAN: Short-term Economic Observatory annual on main Companies in Japan, 1983, Tokyo, Japan.

KYOIKUSHA (Ed.): Business Comparison of Electric Industries, Kyoikusha Publishing Co., 1980, Tokyo, Japan.

NIKKEI MECHANICAL (Ed.): A Guidebook to Mechatronics Japan '84, The Nihon Keizai Shimbun, 1984, Tokyo, Japan.

MONTHLY BULLETIN OF ECONOMIC DEVELOPMENT, No. 161, August 1983, Tokyo, Japan.

MONTHLY LABOR STATISTICS AND RESEARCH BULLETIN, Vol. 35, No. 12, December 1983, Tokyo, Japan.

THE NIKKEI SANGYO SHIMBUN, Sept 1, 1980, Tokyo, Japan.

SAGYO NORITSU COLLEGE (Ed.): Management Annual '82, Publishing Department of Sangyo Noritsu College, 1982, Tokyo, Japan.

II. Articles

WAKUTA, HIROAKI: "Japanese Management in Changing Era and Management Education by Hierarchies in Future", in: STATUS QUO AND PERSPECTIVES OF MANAGEMENT EDUCATIONS; Proceeding of Japan Management Education Society, October, 1981, Tokyo, Japan.

SAITO, TAKENORI: University and Management Education in Modern Japan, Seibundo Publishing Co., 1981, Tokyo, Japan.

WATANABE, SHIGERU: The Era of Regional Technology, Tsusho Sangyo Chosakai, 1982, Tokyo, Japan.

SHIMIZU, SHIGERU: "Education of Company in Transition --- Learn the Case", THE DIAMOND RECRUITE INFORMATION, Vol. 9, No. 6, July/August, 1983, Tokyo, Japan.

KOBAYASHI, SHIGERU: "New Investment Effectiveness Study", in: THE PRODUCTION MATERIAL AND MARKETING, September, 1983, Nagoya, Japan.

Vocational Education and Challenge at a Time of Rapid Technological Change - Considerations on the Dual System

Theodor Dams

Definitions and the Problem

Primary vocational education (generally for 15-18 years-olds) which is carried out in firms and in part-time vocational schools as well as in special training centers not linked with the firms is termed the "dual system".

A OECD-Country study on Education Policy (1971) explained at the time, "the thorough system of vocational training... according to the traditional, firmly established 'dual system', has made Germany famous". Twenty years previously the "Office of the High Commissioner" delivered an equally positive judgement: ("... the system has produced in several areas what are perhaps the best skilled workers in the world, and has achieved great importance in the economic development of the nation".) Up to the present day the "dual system" enjoys the same high reputation in the internal discussion as the term "made in Germany" has attained international trade relations.

Historical Challenges

At present, technological developments are putting increased demands on the qualification structure of the education system. Yet this is not the only time in which changes in the primary vocational education have become necessary or apparent. The "dual system" has undergone decisive changes over time; in its current form it is the product of a process of development stretching back about one hundred years.

1. The traditional apprenticeship system (a corporative society of craft guilds, etc.) began to break up during the course of industrialization. This prompted, for instance, the "Verein für Socialpolitik" to discuss with a great degree of scientific interest the "reform of the apprenticeship system" at its 1875 meeting in Eisenach. At around the turn of the century, the craft regulations were amended, and the apprenticeship training system was reformed (educational institutions and accompanying schooling in addition to on-the-job experience as the basis of preliminary vocational education). The system of vocational schools was greatly expanded in the following decades, and with it the theoretical basis of vocational training was spread.

2. After 1933, a national central policy was established determining all vocational organization, which is still the case today. In cooperation with representatives from the professional associations, technical requirements were established in the form of professional standards, educational regulations, and regulations for the conduct of examinations. Revisions were institutionalized by continuous changes caused by technical advances. This manner of continually revising the educational regulations during rapid technological change has remained up until today as a great challenge for those persons responsible for primary vocational training!

3. In the 1950s, and especially in the 1960s, further reforms were introduced. There were mainly two forms or reasons which led to this:

a) In those areas, in which the "dual system" was not able to satisfy the rising technical-administrative demands of the economy (due to the structure of the training institutions), full-time vocational schools arose to fill the gap. They had, however, still a further function, which was to supply technically higher qualification structure, by making career advancement possible (obtaining the qualifications for access to third-level schooling).

b) The secondary school system was reformed (Level II, from the 11th to the 13th class) or should be reorganized to establish (1) a closer link between the educational and the employment system, and (2) to attain a better transition to the university level through differentiation in the various educational areas.

4. Since the late 1970s, early 1980s the dual system is being confronted by several challenges for which it must find anwers. Partly, they are of a short-term nature, but some are also long-term.

a) The persons born in the years with a very high birth rate (the baby-boom generation) are now entering the educational system, mainly the socondary school level II, (including the dual system) and the universities. The quantitative aspect dominates currently (at times of negative or lower economic growth) which is in this case the question how many young people will be able to find a apprenticeship in a firm. The goal of highest priority in vocational training policy will, therefore, be lowering the unemployment rate for young people, by raising the number of vocational training positions in the handicrafts, industry and in commerce (this is a problem to be solved in the short-term, whereas its urgency will decrease in a few years).

b) Consideration of the technical-organizational changes in the economy and in society in the relevant professions at an early time: this means determining new basic professional requirements as well as drawing up a plan of the vocational qualification structures, (development of curricula, educational regulations, etc.).

c) The possible repercussions of technological, technical and organizational change on the educational
system as a whole, and in particular on the dual
system; this includes for instance the structure of
labor market/of the training situation (unskilled,
semi-skilled workers, qualified workers, a broad basic
education vs. specialization at an early point in
time, etc.)

d) Because the dual system is a matter of contracts for
training positions in the private-sector, the wage
agreements negotiated between the trade unions and the
employers have a direct effect on these private
contracts (for instance, provisions such as shortening
working hours or extending the length of training
time, remuneration during training, etc.). In addition, there are tendencies towards lowering the
barriers created by the child labor laws (see the goal
according to a), and reducing the amount of time spent
in vocational school (theoretical part of the education) to one day a week.

e) Today those necessary (and often sizeable) investments
which take into account the new requirements resulting
from technological developments, should be carefully
planned, because in a few years the number of young
people being trained in the dual system will decrease
considerably (after approximately 1985/86).[1].

Only a concept oriented more towards the long-term
will be able to avoid misdirected investments, which
are already beginning to emerge.

Selection of the problems to be treated

I have intentionally presented a broader overview of the
questions and problems which will or could arise for
vocational training in the dual system in this time of

rapid technological change. In the following, we will deal primarily with two of these areas of inquiry. In the explanation of these, sharp goal conflicts arise between the <u>quantitative</u> problem of increasing the number of persons employed in a training program, <u>and</u> the <u>qualitative</u> aspect of a new approach or reorientation with regard to the contents.

No definitive results can be presented for the latter problem yet; in addition to the question of securing an institutional basis for development of the curriculum, an overview of current research being conducted will be presented. Altogether, there are more questions that remain open than could already be answered in this difficult area of primary first vocational training.

The quantitative problem and qualitative conclusions

According to the particular age groups (average age 15-16 years), the proportion of those persons having a contract for training amounts to 55,6 % (1977) or 61,6 % (1982) (from 1.005 million or 1.015 million young persons total). These numbers prove that a) the dual system is even today still a "pillar" of primary first vocational training; and b) adjustment processes in this areas of education are of great importance for the competitiveness of the economy, c) in spite of the difficult economic situation, the number of trainee positions in the firms could be increased.[2]

The situation on the labor market is assessed differently by the government, the employers, and the trade unions. The federal government comes to the conclusion: "The dual system has stood the test". The German Trade Union Federation: "In the year 1983, the situation for young people seeking training was critical, such as it has rarely been before. Once again, the right to education was not realized".

The Vocational Training Report 1984 showed that in 1983 approximately 80,000 young people did not receive a trainee position; two-thirds of them were girls. For 1984 it is estimated that the demand for trainee positions will reach 730,000 (In 1983 677,700 persons were able to sign trainee contracts). The number of persons who do not receive a trainee position will very probably increase. - At the same time, the question how to help young women and the physically handicapped to find qualified training will become more critical.

There is also the problem of a regional "lack of supply" in the dual system. In addition, the number of young persons who have completed their apprenticeship and who are unable to find a job, is increasing.

It is important to mention in this context: (1) Classifying the training positions according to branch or sector leads one to assume that so-called misstructuring has increased (divergence between being trained for an occupation, and later practicing that vocation); i.e. that after completion of training, problems of retraining for another vocation or of unemployment will arise. (2) It is a well-known phenomenon that the quality of on-the-job training in the firms differs greatly; one can assume that with an increase in the number of apprenticeships being offered during the recession, the quality of the training certainly did not increase. (3) According to comprehensive surveys, the net training costs of the firms are considerable; this could lead to a reluctance to hire on the part of those employers, whose earnings base is less favorable, or who train young persons in the "modern" occupations entailing high costs. (4) One cannot overlook the fact that the federal and state governments in the Federal Republic of Germany have financed special programs, in order to create additional training positions in the firms; therefore, the government finances increasingly the primary vocational training, which is actually in contradiction to the character of the dual system.

These few remarks adequately should illustrate that employment problems under the conditions of rapid technological change have an effect on a historically traditional educational system - especially at times of recession or for the generation of young people born in years of high birth rates.

Institutional aspects of considering and compiling new contents of the training program

The regulations for primary vocational education for firms are issued as administrative orders by the Federal Minister for the Economy in agreement with the Federal Minister for Education and Science. With regard to the professional qualification structures at a time of rapid technological change, two facts are of importance: (a) it is extremely difficult to estimate ex-ante the future qualification requirements for a job, and to integrate them into the curriculum; and (b) the technical experience of the firms, as well as the findings of the researchers on vocational training should be drawn upon when preparing new regulations for training.

Previous to the issuance of an administrative order or an educational regulation by the responsible Federal Ministry, an institutionally secured advisory and preparatory process begins: The Federal Institute for Research on Vocational Training (Bundesinstitut für Berufsbildungsforschung) discusses the content of the primary vocational training with experts from the trade associations (employers) and the appropriate trade union, in agreement with the basic plan of instruction of the Permanent Conference of Ministers of Education of the States (for the vocational schools).

The counterpart to the institutionally secured preparation of new training regulations is their use and testing
in the Vocational Education Committees of the Chambers of
Commerce or the Chambers of Handicrafts, in which
management and labor are represented.

This institutional-administrative decision-making process
on the new educational regulations can be seen as an
hinderance in the process between management and labor
towards clarifying the content of instruction; however,
it can also be seen as positive that the experiences and
new technological knowledge of the firms can be directly
and systematically translated into the primary vocational
training through new or revised educational regulations.

Results of studies with general objectives

The studies specifically prepared in the Federal Republic
go back to the results of studies done by international
organizations - in particular the OECD. They were
especially concerned with the effects of microelectronics
and robots on the labor market; we refer here to the
OECD-studies on Japan, Sweden, and the FR Germany[3].

From these specific studies, dealing with the effects of
new technologies on the educational system, we can deduce
the following results:

1. The classical manpower-approach continues up until
today in the "modern qualifications research" on vocational training; besides this there is the "flexibility
research" approach and the strategies to convey a supply
of higher qualifications, which in turn affects the
qualification requirements (U. Grünewald).

2. The requirements for professional qualifications are
raised by the new technologies (BDI); this holds true
when the available jobs are expected to remain constant.

(Prognos/Mackintosh) in regard to the "increasing need for more highly qualified and flexibly usable personell. .. this applies particularly to employees with vocational training, whose area of assignment is very broad..." Because of the worsening situation on the labor market (up til 1985: plus 600,000 persons employed), "policy measures on the labor market will become necessary, so for instance mobility assistance, support for recurrent vocational education, retraining, etc.".

3. According to interviews with experts and surveys of firms, 54 occupations are particularly affected both quantitatively and qualitatively by microprocessor/ microcomputer technologies (MP/MC). 0.5 million trainees were employed in these areas, which is one-third of the total number of trainees (Gizycki/Weiler); the individual occupations are affected differently.

4. The empirical investigations show that positive demand exists in the electrical and electronic professions due to MP/MC technology, there is stagnation or a decrease in demand for the commercial and administrative professions, as well as in the metal industry (Gizycki/Weiler).

5. The altered content of the requirements will be particularly strong for the electrical occupations. For all of the occupations mentioned above, the qualifications for entry are gaining increased importance. ("abstract, theoretical thinking, ability to plan, creativity, ability to communicate, ability for team-work (E. Hofmeister). This has consequences: (a) for the school-leaving certificates; (b) for the educational objectives of the part-time vocational schools.

6. In the dual system it is the role of the vocational schools to reconsider the content of what is being taught, and to critically reflect on the coordination and conveyance of vocational qualifications in the firm. The vocational schools do not fulfill today's requirements.

7. Recurrent vocational education is becoming more important than ever before, it takes place increasingly in the firms, in the institutions supported either by the firms themselves or by the trade unions, and in the publicly financed institutions.

The conclusions from these general investigations: They all remain in very general terms; in principle, they do not differ very much from the results and ideas that were presented by the German Education Council at the beginning of the 1970s. The concrete consideration of technological change in the formulation of concrete educational regulations thus necessitates increased applied research. It is conducted by research institutes specially created for that purpose through legislation. In both of the institutes, the research programs of which are summarized below (as far as they are relevant to the topic), the employers and the unions are represented, as well as the federal and state governments.

Areas of emphasis in vocational training research at a time of rapid technological change

The discussion on new content of instruction can be freed of its emotional associations when the facts of the matter themselves are objectified through vocational training research. In addition to the great number of university institutes and research institutes outside the universities, there are in particular two research establishments, which are of primary interest in the context mentioned above:

1) the Bundesinstitut für Berufsbildung, Berlin/Bonn (Federal Institute for Vocational Education), an institution in accordance with the Vocational Training Act;
2) the Institut für Arbeitsmarkt- und Berufsforschung der

Bundesanstalt für Arbeit (the Institute for Labor
Market and Vocational Research of the Federal Labor
Office).

Both have different functions, corresponding to their
particular institutional classification. The results of
each one's work, however, supplements very well that of
the other, in order to arrive at an overall judgement on
the problem.

Research Emphasis of the Bundesinstitut für Berufsbildung

Judging from those educational regulations which have
been recently revised, there seems to be a tendency "to
adapt them to the technical developments", and to
integrate the use of "modern machines", rather than
presenting fundamentally new occupational conceptions. -
Initially the emphasis in this respect lies on research
projects with a longer-term orientation. They can be
chäracterized under the heading "technical-organizational
change":

a) effects of technical-organizational change on the
   qualification requirements of the employment system

b) microelectronics and vocational training state of art
   developments of the empirical research and consequences for vocational education

c) influence of · information technologies on recurrent
   commercial education

d) recurrent education in the area of technical computer
   sciences

e) effects of microprocessor technology on the qualification process in the occupations dealing with metal
   technology and electrotechnology (media, forms for
   imparting information, proposals for structuring)

f) testing the use of correspondence courses in recurrent

education in the area of "programming and use of numerically controlled machines for production"

g) the qualification contributions for the use of micro-computers in small and middle-sized firms.

The results of such studies should, first, be integrated into the curricula of the directly affected occupations; they should also be taken into account when revising the professions in general. The applied research studies mentioned above are being used in certain occupations (1983: approximately 90 occupations; 1984/85: approx. 50) in "Structures and Contents of Courses of Training". The continuation of these studies leads to research projects on the subject "development of educational media" and also in reflections on "educating the educators".

In the context of the strong informational orientation of this paper, I will have to refrain from making an interpretation of the studies; in the area of micro-electronics and microprocessors, the studies which are relevant for preliminary vocational first education, advanced training, and recurrent training have not yet been completed.

The Institute for Labor Market and Occupational Research (IAB) of the Federal Agency of Labor (Institut für Arbeitsmarkt- und Berufsforschung (IAB) der Bundesanstalt für Arbeit

The actual area of concentration of the research studies is in the labor market. In the context of this paper, three areas are of primary importance:

1) the structure of occupations and qualifications research;
2) flexibility research;
3) technical developments and their effects on the labor market.

In addition to the more general studies, the IAB has increasingly investigated aspects of the labor market (and thereby vocational training).

In 1982 the 4th special program was presented with the title "Challenges for the Labor Market and Occupational Research 1983-97". Several of the theses supported there are listed below, as far as they are particularly relevant to the topic:

1. The structural change in the education and employment systems demands additional adaptability from all participants.

2. Only qualifications and employment for those persons born in the years of high birth rates (baby-boom generation) can guarantee a secure future for all.

3. Will technical change really become a threat?

4. Occupational research must take new roads when depicting and defining the occupations and activities.

The research program shows clearly a stronger emphasis on investigations on the connections between technical change and developments in the labor market, as well as the consequences for vocational education that are involved.

Concluding Remarks

These seminars, as part of the Nagoya-Freiburg cooperation, persue among other things the goal to provide information on specific economic problems which are relevant for both countries: Information on existing institutions and existing problems is the first step in gaining an understanding for the questions of "the other side".

This article attempted to point out the problems which arise for primary vocational first training as a result of increased technical change: As a traditional educational system, the "dual system" has certainly proved itself in the past, but is coming under increased pressure: technical change alters the situation in the labor market and makes vocational qualifications necessary - economic recession or stagnation limits the absorption capacity of the firms to employ new trainees for a qualifying primary vocational training position, and the baby-boom generation is crowding into the training courses provided by the firms. In view of these aspects, the "dual system" will have to stand the test in the years to come; carefully directed and applied research can substantially ease this process or reorientation, if it is completed in time.

Footnotes:

1) An estimate by the Permanent Conference for Education
Ministers of the States cited the following numbers of
people from the secondary level I: 1984 - 764,000;
1985 - 715,000; 1987 - 616,000 and 1990 - 499,000.

2) In 1982, 25,000 more persons entered training programs
than in the previous year (+4.2%), from 631,057 total;
in the following year (1982) demand exceeded supply by
14,185 places (-2.1%).

3) Other members of the seminar will report on the
development of the labor market.

The Structure of the Education System in the Federal Republic of Germany

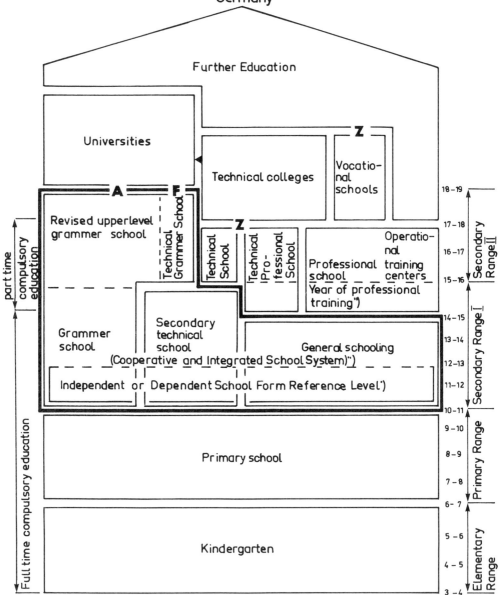

Source : Minister of Science and Education, Govermental Report on the structural problems in the federal education system, Bonn 1978, p. 7

Legend : A = general certificate of education F = technical certificate of education Z = technical school certificate of education

') not found in all states; partly experimental education projects

'') not valid for all students or trainees

Technological Development and the Labor Market in Light of the Differential Social Structures in Japan and the Federal Republic of Germany

Kunihiro Jojima

1 The Problem

Industrial nations today recognize that technological progress brings prosperity to some, while disturbing the social order of others. The dominating influence depends on the circumstances involved; it is these circumstances in Japan and in the Federal Republic of Germany which should be closely examined.

The complexity of technological progress calls for synthesis of its elements in order to support the division of labor. This is, however, a logical contradiction to the dynamics of technological and cultural development. The question of how to logically overcome this difficulty must be viewed in relationship to the social dynamic, which is measured according to the sluggishness of the lifestyle; in this case conservative. The fact that the lifestyle cannot always keep up with the rapid technological changes evidences the "time lag" problematic.

Actually, technological progress is dependent on contemporary ideology. The ideology, in a long term view, is not constant, but changes in direction and interdependant with other developments. An example is seen in present day Iran, where a reverse in the direction of technological "development" is being witnessed.

In this article a discussion of the various questions which have been briefly mentioned will be directed towards employment problems, with regard to the differences in the social frame-works of Japan and the Fed. Republic of Germany.

2 A Logical Classification for Technological Development

Technological development can be divided into three areas
in regard to the division of labor between capital an
labor:

1) Labor is completely replaced (a technological proress
   which saves labor)

2) Old technologies are replaced (saving e.g. time,
   energy, raw materials)

3) Labor is not replaced (e.g. the replacement of walking
   by the automobile).

The standard employment problem lies in the quantity of
labor, which is covered above in the first two areas.
Fluctuations in the demand for labor develop mostly as a
result of the law of equilization regarding value of
marginal production for capital and labor, causing
overemployment, full employment, or unemployment. In
order to achieve the desired result of full employment,
the regulation of wages and interest rates would be
necessary. Such management measures are clearly identi-
fied as a trade cycle policy.

Additionally, lowering the effective interest rate
through technological progress via increased capital
productivity is a possibility that could be categorized
in either the first, second, or both areas.

In light of these considerations, the following conclusion can be drawn: The second category lies in a "gray
area" because it overlaps with the first and third. Also,
it would be altogether dispensable in an analysis of the
main role of technological development.

A new type of technological development, falling in the third category as a supplement, focuses on creating jobs, especially within the tertiary sector. Full employment accounts today for the cardinal problem in industrial nations because labor-saving technology causes mass unemployment, which cannot be adequately subdued by the primary and secondary sectors. In Japan the labor- saving technological progress is accompanied by an enormous and unavoidable growth in the tertiary sector. (Japan's tertiary sector has increased from 29,7 % in 1950 to 55,3 % in 1980 - Practically doubling in 30 years.)

The final conclusion, which calls for a logical differentiation of the main purpose and roles, provides three different types of technological development (TD):

a) TD (a) which replaces labor (category 1)
b) TD (b) which does not replace labor (category 3)
c) TD (c) which does not replace capital

Each pair of these three categories is then, in the case of full employment, in a supplementary relationship that cannot be replaced. This statement can be thus presented:

$$TD\ (a) + TD\ (b) = K_1$$
$$TD\ (b) + TD\ (c) = K_2$$
$$TD\ (c) + TD\ (a) = K_3 \quad (K_1,\ K_2,\ K_3 \text{ are constants})$$

In that the three build a type of closed system, it can be understood that there is no other type of technological development on this abstract level.

3   Technological Development which replaces labor

TD is essentially dependent on the social structure which
is connected to the wage system. In Japan as well as in
the Fed. Rep. of Germany, the alterations in wages and a
trade cycle policy are used as management measures. In
comparison, Japan's wages are essentially more elastic.
On the national average, 50 % of all salaries are paid as
a bonus, which is relatively flexible, according to the
trade cycle. Also, labor unions in Japan are more
adaptable to fluctuations in trade than are their
counterparts in Germany.

Furthermore, because company managements usually operate
under the "family principle", a "lay-off" system remains
foreign to Japan. This institutional characteristic has
been successful in alleviating opposition to the newly
introduced labor-saving technologies, while Germany has
experienced more opposition. "Mitbestimmung" can be
recognized as a substitute for the family principle.

Japan has another special feature, in that it has no
foreign workers. Since the end of World War II foreign
workers have not been allowed to immigrate into Japan.
The resulting shortage of workers who were willing to do
unpopular jobs had to be countered by engaging labor-
saving capital. This stimulated the TD (a) within
labor-saving during the era of the "economic miracle".
Through this action, and due to a dependency on the
advanced qualification in the education system, the
number of native workers who were able to adapt to
unpopular jobs decreased. (40 % of all youth attend
highschool, and almost 90 % earn their diploma). Young
people are often too proud of their education to engage
in simple occupations. The structual inbalance on this
level of labor is a mandate to TD (a), which can sufficiently alleviate this problem.

In spite of existing motivation, such cases are not
always profitable. In the 70's a great deal of capital
was exported in order to secure simple and cheap labor. A
bumerang effect was felt, however, as the domestic
textile industry suffered a slup. At the end of the 70's,
though, a reversal in this process came about through an
automation boom. Capital returned and Japan's exports
increased. This was caused by filling gaps in the
different labor levels through automation from TD (a).

In the long run, such a development is not always welcomed because Japan's export surplus can not be balanced
through the capital transfer, and developing nations
(with the exception of those rich in raw materials)
suffer from a lack of currency. The reversal caused by TD
(a) led to a situation in world trade in which the
circulation of capital and goods on the global level can
no longer be closed. World trade has also been influenced
by extremely high interest rates in the U.S., which have
attracted foreign investment, bringing more profit than
that of a direct investment in most countries. TD (a) is
still welcomed today in Japan, and its meaning has not
yet been associated with "job alienation".

As for areas of difference between Japan and Europe,
social structure is a good starting point. In comparison
to Japan, social class mobility in Europe and job status
are relatively low. In Japan the difference between blue
collar and white collar workers is not as clear as it is
in Europe.

The rapid automation in Japan could not have been possible in Europe due to the fact that surplus labor could
not have been absorbed. Also, the introduction of
automation is problematic in Germany because of the lack
of regional mobility for employers.

In my opinion, the following conclusions can be made concerning the development of automation: In Japan the development is more favorable and runs smoother than in Germany. Japan faces the danger, though, of being reckless and short-sighted in its implementation of automation. In the same way, the law of equilization is only considered valid for this type of technological progress.

4 Technological Development which does not replace labor

The function and role of a car, for instance, cannot be replaced by human labor today. It is the same case with the capabilities of large computers; these types of technological development belong to category TD (b).

Thus far there is no model for TD (b), which can show what future developments should be. Although it has made incredible contributions to society, it has simultaneously burdened humanity with problems of great magnitude, as seen in environmental pollution. There are many who fear a future that is determined by increased TD (b), but they fail to supply a political model for an alternative culture.

It appears to be necessary then to provide a suitable model for TD (b). This is found in the entirety of the three TD as expressed in the three formulas. Capital and labor do not always comply with the law as stated in economic theory, but rather they comply with the realm enclosed in the three formulas - even though as to date no calculation method has been found.

One prerequisite for the maintenance of this model is full employment. The demand of full employment does not, however, secure an optimal combination of the three TD.

5 Technological Development where Capital cannot be replaced - TD that creates Labor

In the course of the stampeding automation in Japan, an occasional "no ones' factory" will crop up, in which the workers have disappeared. The company has switched employees from jobs replaced by automation to jobs in sales, and has reduced hiring quotas. Such factories are balanced out by the present growth in Japan's "soft industry" or tertiary sector. The goal of TD (c) consists especially in serving the expansion of the "soft industry".

Soft industries are characterized by their low capital investment. Industries falling under this classification would be: the information industry, tutoring schools, care centers for young and old, and other services.

Thanks to flourishing soft industries, Japan finds itself today in the age of passivity. Everything is inevitably provided and prepared without observing the process or having to ask for it. This kind of comfort may not be without disadvantages. TD (c) now extends into the area of everyday household work. Although TD (c) has greatly relieved the housewife of toilsome and burdensome housework, it has also led to the reduction of her role within the family. The children no longer know, for example, how a real homecooked meal tastes because dinner comes already prepared from the store. Children today can use a pocket calculator without having to understand the rules of calculation. It is no longer necessary to think and consider because machines have stored entire thought processes. Such developments have brought about a structural passivity that is now noticeable in Japan. Too much is also too little.

Along with the externalization of the household work,

additional expenses have come. This has produced a multitude of "emancipated" housewifes who work parttime in order to make up for the extra costs.

Moreover, education costs have risen due to the fact that society today requires a higher level of education in order for a child to obtain a reasonable job when he is finished. A highschool education runs as high as 150,000 DM in Japan. The birthrate in Japan has decreased from 28,1 (per 1000) in 1950 to 13,6 in 1980, during which time the rate in Germany fell from 28,1 to 10,1. This trend also results from the fact that parents can no longer expect to be supported by their children when they reach old age. Although a halt to the population decrease appears improbable, it is necessary to undertake measures against it. Such a view represents the search for an optimal combination of the three TD.

6 Closing Remarks

TD is categorized into just three types: TD (a), (h), and (c), which create a closed system (given full employment). This means that each pair of the three TD are closed in regard to the division of labor (the supplementation relationship is irreplaceable). Due to the impact of TD on human life, it is imperative that it be guided by basic and fundamental points. One is the family as a fundamental nucleus. This view makes sense in light of the "family principle", which is the source of all social obligation in government and business. Social security and peace are endangered due to the fact that the faily nucleus is breaking down and can no longer fulfill its role as an example.

The extended family (as seen in China, Korea, or possibly Italy) fails to adjust to economic development. The over-emphasis on family ties leads to a situation in which people are not able to recognize the necessity of a higher order in the social system, and from which nepotism and local patriotism develop.

Industrial nations suffer today from the anti-social activities of their young people. This is another result of the break down of the family nucleus. Most of the countries tend to be socialized states whose finance structure continues to be burdened by the externalization of household work. This process is accompanied in Japan by the swell in the soft industry, which is for the purpose of attaining a seemingly full employment. Everything which has been presented above - the family nucleus, family ties, the extreme reduction in the birthrate, the externalization of household work, the weaking of social ties, the anti-social conduct of youth, the lack of qualified labor, the over-expansion of the soft industry, the over burdening of public finances - all of these move in a vicious circle.

The solution to this nightmare is to reverse the tendency by using full employment to balance the three TD. A collective intervention policy is necessary because isolated measures are not effective.

It would be appropriate, then, to subdue the TD (a) while accelerating TD (b). In this case, while the constant K remains constant in regard to the supplementation relationship between the two TD, the absolute standard size of K can be changed at will.

This results in:

$$K_1 + K_2 - 2 \text{ TD (b)} = K_3$$

$$K_2 + K_3 - 2 \text{ TD (c)} = K_1$$

$$K_3 + K_1 - 2 \text{ TD (a)} = K_2 \quad \text{so,}$$

$$\text{TD (a)} + \text{TD (c)} + 2 \text{ TD (b)} = K_1 + K_2$$

When $K_2 + K_1$ is given, the intervention policy mentioned
above is possible in conjunction with the reduction of TD
(c). It is clear that a fundamental TD policy must come
from the advancement of TD (b). This policy would offer a
solution to the question of employment, which is, in
seemingly full employment the lack of qualified labor, or
spontaneous unemployment. It must be emphasized that the
question of employment in industrial nations is in no way
adequately answered in full employment.

On the other hand, the development of TD (b) is also
limited, in that the three TD are even under "given"
conditons at some time a closed system. This is due to
the fact that K_1, K_2, and K_3 are actually to be viewed as
constants for the total system.

The system can alter according to subsequent conditon
changes. These conditons are not only objective, but are
instead dependent upon the view of those on the outside,
the contemporary ideology. With a new ideology come now
developments in TD (b). In this sense TD (b) is never
ending.

From a neutral standpoint, it can be considered as to
whether TD (b) is passing man by in its development. It
can also bring weighty disadvantages with it: Industrialization at the cost of the environment, increased
income at the cost of population growth, city comfort at
the cost of country peacefulness, etc..

Science has no answers in regard to what tomorrow's
ideology will be. Concerning thoughts on TD; the greatest
importance lies within the relationship between the
direction of development and the question of employment.

A Report on the Scientific Cooperation
Between the Economics Faculty of Freiburg University
and Japan, Specifically Nagoya University

1. Preliminary Remarks

At the opening of Japan to the outside world in the last
century a rapid expansion was experienced in the academic
relationship between Japan and Germany. Japan used German
research and teaching for its own development in not only
law and medicine, but in economics and agronomy as well.

In this century, especially after WW II, these contacts
lost their intensity. Talented young Japanese economists
tended to learn English and thus became more interested in
the teaching methods and economic and social research of
the English-speaking world.

With this background, it has been a deep concern of the
Economics Faculty of Freiburg University since the 1960s
to create a new platform through a continuous expansion of
contacts. The main objectives are:

- to supply information about the state of the German
  economy and its economic science to East Asia, and

- to gather information about Japan's economic development
  and policy, which are of increasing importance in the
  world.

2. Institutional Cooperation

2.1 Contacts with the Economics Faculty of Nagoya University

For the faculty in Freiburg, the scientific cooperation
with the Economics Faculty of Nagoya University is the

most important activity relating to Japan. Nagoya University, now a state university (kokuritsu daigaku), was one of the few imperial universities (founded prior to WW II). It has an outstanding reputation in Japan. Close scientific contacts have been intact now for more than 10 years, having found their most visible expression in the regularly organized joint seminars.

Since 1977, a seminar has taken place each year alternately in Nagoya and in Freiburg. The participating economists read papers on a defined range of subjects. The major goal is to inform the partner on specific issues and circumstances in the other country, as well as to brief the partner on the present state of research in these areas. This exchange of information provides an orientation for the partner country through which mutual learning processes become possible.

The following subjects have been addressed in the previous ten seminars. (Their content will be more closely outlined in section 5.1).

1977 (Nagoya)	Problems in Spatial Economic Development and Regional Economic Policy Issues in Japan and the Federal Republic of Germany (FRG)
1978 (Freiburg)	Development Policy - Technology Transfer - Foreign Investment
1979 (Nagoya)	Economic Adjustment Processes under Uncertainty (Recession, Inflation)
1980 (Freiburg)	Current Social Policy Problems in Japan and in the FRG
1981 (Nagoya)	Economic Adjustment Problems Due to Rising Energy Prices in Japan and in the FRG
1982 (Freiburg)	International Economic Relations: Japan - European Community - Federal Republic of Germany
1983 (Nagoya)	Decision Processes on the Micro- and Macroeconomic Levels

1984 (Freiburg)   Employment Problems under the Conditions
                  of Rapid Technological Change

1985 (Nagoya)   Structural Developments and Economic and
                  Political Conditions in Japan and the FRG

1986 (Freiburg)   The   Role   of   Japan   and   the   Federal
                  Republic of Germany in the World Economy
                  - with Special Reference to Small and
                  Medium-Sized Companies

planned:
1988 (Nagoya)   Protectionism vs. Liberalization

The 10-15 papers discussed in each seminar - half of them
written by Germans, half by Japanese - provide a broad
range of issues and opinions. As for paper selection, a
wide range of approaches is valued: various methodological
standpoints (empirical work vs. theoretical examination),
different levels of reflection (macroeconomic vs. micro-
economic analysis), and thesis (factual information vs.
examination of theories vs. policy analysis and recommen-
dation).

Lecturers thus far have included acknowledged specialists
as well as younger researchers from the host university;
in this manner the latter were given an early opportunity
in international dialogue. The participation of speakers
from two other universities in the Nagoya vicinity (Chubu
and Nanzan in 1984) indicates the wide interest in the
seminars.

In the fall of 1986, the 10th Joint Seminar took place. In
celebration of the 10 year anniversary, it was commenced
with a special one day colloquium open to the public.
Representatives from German enterprises in Japan and from
Japanese enterprises in Germany spoke on the topic
"Managing Enterprises in Japan and in the Federal Republic
of Germany". The lively discussion that followed clearly
showed the public interest in the cooperation of Japan and
Germany.

In addition to the joint seminars, visiting researchers had the opportunity to become acquainted with the practices of the host country, its business, and governmental administration. The participation of hosts and guests provided - in comparison to normal factory tours - the opportunity for a fruitful exchange of ideas on specific issues.

One important component of the contact with Nagoya is the "Economic Research Center" at its Economics Faculty, which is equipped with its own library and computer system. The center publishes books and discussion papers, in which, among others, various articles stemming from the cooperation with Freiburg have been published. There is special interest in questions on small and medium enterprises. In the meantime, this institution has opened its doors to scientists from Freiburg (Dr. W. Pascha, Oct. 1986 - June 1987).

2.2 Further Institutional Contacts

In addition to the cooperation with Nagoya, further contacts to other Japanese institutions have developed. In part, the cooperation with Nagoya worked as a catalyst. For example, good relations have developed with Chubu University in Nagoya, which has opened a department for international studies in the wake of a nationwide trend of "internationalization". Furthermore, contacts with the Central Agricultural Co-operative of Aichi in Nagoya are being continued. In mid 1985 the Institute for Development Policy (IFEP), which is an extention of the Freiburg faculty, assisted a managerial representative on an information trip through Germany. In the fall of 1985 the director of IFEP, Prof. Dams, visited the co-operative. In the fall of 1986 the president and several department managers of the co-operative were welcomed in Freiburg for informative talks. The delegation not only visited agricultural enterprises and various co-operatives, but also the Badischer Genossenschaftsverband (Karlsruhe) in order to gain further information about co-operatives in Germany.

In the last decade, contacts made by Freiburg scientists in the area of agronomy have been taken up again, including those which had been made before WW II and in the early fifties (especially through Dr. C. von Dietze, Institute of Agronomy).

The renewed contacts made by C. von Dietze in the 1950's have been intensified especially since 1970. In this respect, the many years of activity by Professor Dams on the board of the International Association of Agricultural Economists, including his IAAE presidency 1979-82 and collaboration with vice-president K. Ohkawa/ Tokyo over many years, also provided a favorable basis. Additionally, a number of close institutional and personal contacts exist with the agro-economic professorship at the state universities (Tokyo, Kyoto, Nagoya, etc.) and respected private universities. The presence of German agro-economics has made a recovery especially in Nagoya, and even in development policy and economic history (Dr. K. Jojima, Dr. T. Matsugi, Dr. H. Fujise). Economists in Freiburg, on the other hand, are presently completing a scientific paper on Japanese agricultural policy.

Furthermore, there are connections to the International Development Center of Japan (IDCJ), Tokyo, and especially to its research director, K. Ohkawa. Further contacts have been made to the newly founded International University of Japan. Its president, S. Okita, a former Foreign Minister of Japan and Director of the Japanese Economic Growth Center, as well as Head of the Japanese Loan Institution for Development Aid, has been a good cooperation partner for many years. Furthermore, there are relations to the Nanzan University (Nagoya), to the economics faculty at Sophia University (Tokyo), to the Center for Southeast Asian Studies at Kyoto University, and to the United Nations Center for Regional Development (UNCRD) in Nagoya.

3. Personnel Exchange

3.1 Stays by Faculty Members from Nagoya University in Freiburg

In addition to joint research work (within the framework of the joint seminars), the exchange of professors and doctoral students has provided the cornerstone for the relationship of the two universities.

Various professors from Nagoya have stayed in Freiburg for long periods of research. They were supported by their Freiburg colleagues.

- Dr. Dr. K. Jojima   several times, last visited in 1983 for 6 months; scholarships from the Alexander von Humboldt Foundation

- Dr. T. Matsugi   several times, last visited in 1984 for 3 months, stayed three years at the beginning of the seventies; A. von Humboldt Scholarship

- Dr. A. Iida   in 1978 for three months; DAAD scholarship

Other professors visited Freiburg for shorter stays:

- Dr. M. Mizuno   (1978)
- Dr. N. Okuno   (1980)
- Dr. T. Makido   (1980, 1985)

Furthermore, numerous postgraduate students from Nagoya have been supervised by the Freiburg faculty since 1973. They usually did research for one or two years, supported by scholarships from the Japanese government, DAAD and German foundations:

K. Yagi, M.A.

T. Kishi, M.A.

N. Asanuma, M.A.

S. Ito, M.A.

K. Toyota, M.A.

Yoshiki Ohta, M.A.

H. Uchida, M.A.

J. Chikada, M.A.

M. Ban, M.A.

H. Fujimura, M.A.

Yoshiyuki Ohta, M.A.

T. Kato, M.A.

T. Harada, M.A. - presently in Freiburg

N. Fukuzawa, M.A. - presently in Freiburg

Mr. Harada will soon publish the results of his research
on German Idealism and Romanticism and their role in the
history of German economic thought. He is supervised by
Prof. Dr.Dr.h.c. Karl Brandt.

3.2 Stays of other Japanese Guests in Freiburg

Contacts to other places were also cultivated. At the
Business Seminar (Chair Professor Dr. R.-B. Schmidt) the
following visiting professors stayed:

- Dr. Y. Tominaga,   the end of the seventies
  Tokyo University   and beginning of the eighties, 1/2
                          year each time

- Dr. A. Yoshida,   1978/79,
  Yokohama University   approx. 1/2 year.

The following guests stayed for longer periods:

At the Institute for Development Policy:

- Dr. A. Tokiwa, Keio University, Tokyo; 1980-82
- Dr. M. Kaneko, Meiji University, Tokyo; 1982-83
- Dr. Y. Takei, Shizuoka University; 1985 for 1 month

At the Economics Faculty:

- T. Masuzawa, Meiji University, Tokyo; mid 1986 - August 1987

3.3 Stays by Freiburg Faculty Members in Japan

The following members of the Economics Faculty of Freiburg University spent long periods of time in Nagoya (disregarding Nagoya seminar meetings):

- Dr. Dres. h.c. Th. Dams	during the seventies for longer research stays, as well as for several short stays
- Dr. W. Pascha	2 years of research (1982-84); scholarship from the Japanese Ministry of Education (Monbusho). 9 months (1986-87) as a Visiting Research Fellow at the Economic Research Center
- H. J. Laabs	2 1/2 years of research (1984-86); scholarship from the Japanese Ministry of Education (Monbusho)
- U. Schmid	Approx. 2 years of research; presently in Nagoya (since October 1986); scholarship from the Japanese Ministry of Education (Monbusho)
- A. Bernhard	Research stay in Nagoya to begin in January 1988; scholarship from the Japanese Ministry of Education (Monbusho)

Three younger economists went to Japan with DAAD programs:

- Th. Grotowski   1984-86; in Tokyo
- Dr. U. Fischer   1985-87; in Tokyo
- Th. Seidel   1985-87; in Tokyo

4. Teaching

In addition to the intensive scientific contacts between the Economics Faculties, general interest in the partner country increased.

Between October 1985 and February 1986 lectures on "Modern Japan and Germany" were held at the University of Freiburg. The following professors from different faculties contributed their viewpoints on this topic:

- Prof. Dr. Bernd Martin
- Prof. Dr. Karl Kroeschell
- Prof. Dr. Werner Wenz
- Prof. Dr. Arnold Vogt
- Prof. Dr. Theodor Dams
- Prof. Dr. Maria Naumann
- Prof. Dr. Walther Manshard
- Prof. Dr. Takashi Oshio (guest speaker)

A new dimension was added to scientific cooperation when Prof. Dr. Ralf-Bodo Schmidt (Business Economics) taught at Nagoya University in the spring of 1987. During his stay in Nagoya, Schmidt was able to make several contacts for a probable joint research program in the field of business economics.

5.   Publications

5.1 Publications from the Nagoya-Freiburg Dialogue

The cooperation between Nagoya and Freiburg has also resulted in a number of publications. The papers presented in the joint seminar were published in Germany and in Japan. In Germany the following five volumes appeared in the German language; the sixth volume is published in English (Duncker & Humblot; Berlin).

Dams, Theodor/ Jojima, Kunihiro (Ed.)	Ausgewählte Probleme inter-natio-naler Wirtschaftsbeziehungen aus der Sicht Japans und der Bundes-republik Deutschland. Berlin 1980. Focus on: Foreign Direct Invest-ment (Korea, Philippines, etc.), Technology Transfer, Internatio-nal Economic Relations (North-South-Problem, Development Aid, World Monetary System, etc.)
Dams, Theodor/ Jojima, Kunihiro (Ed.)	Aktuelle Probleme der Sozial-politik in Japan und der Bundes-republik Deutschland. Berlin 1982. Focus on: Consequences of the Change in Family Structures, The System of Social Security, Social Security in Agriculture, Social Policy
Dams, Theodor/ Jojima, Kunihiro (Ed.)	Wirtschaftliche Anpassungspro-bleme bei steigenden Energieprei-sen in Japan und der Bundesrepu-blik Deutschland. Berlin 1983. Focus on: Theoretical, Eco-Poli-tical, and Operational Aspects of Economics, Especially with Regard to Economic Adjustment Processes
Dams, Theodor/ Jojima, Kunihiro (Ed.)	Internationale Wirtschaftsbezieh-ungen Japan - Europäische Gemein-schaften - Bundesrepublik Deutschland. Berlin 1983 Focus on: A Continuation of the Discussion of the 1980 Volume, especially World Trade, North-North-Conflicts, Competiveness; World Agra-Market, Issuing Bank Policy

Dams, Theodor/ Mizuno, Masaichi (Ed.)	Entscheidungsprozesse auf mikro- und makroökonomischer Ebene - dargestellt an ausgewählten Beispielen in Japan und in der Bundesrepublik Deutschland. Berlin 1985 Focus on: Decision Processes in Monetary and Fiscal Policy, Structural Adjustment, Use of Quantitative Methods
Dams, Theodor/ Mizuno, Masaichi (Ed.)	Employment Problems under the Conditions of Rapid Technological Change. Berlin 1987 Focus on: Adjustment Problems of Labor Markets through Technological Innovation on the Micro- and Macroeconomic Levels

Future publications will be made in English in order to make the seminar findings accessible to scholars outside Germany.

As for Japan, eight volumes have been published thus far in Japanese.

Mention must also be made of work achieved outside of seminar contacts. During his last stay in Freiburg (1983), Professor Jojima produced the manuscript of his book:

Jojima, K.: Ökonomie und Physik - Eine neue Dimension interdisziplinärer Reflektion, Berlin 1985

Japanese doctoral students have published the results of their Freiburg research in Japanese journals. Dr. Pascha from Freiburg has published, among other papers, the study:

Pascha, W.: Strukturanpassung in schrumpfenden Branchen - Japans Textilindustrie vor dem Hintergrund veränderter Wettbewerbsvorteile. Berlin 1986

It is particularly encouraging that two younger members from Nagoya and Freiburg have collaborated in their research to produce the following joint papers:

Harada, T./ Das "Softnomics-Konzept" des japanischen
Pascha, W. Finanzministeriums: Grundlagen und Anwendung auf die internationalen Wirtschaftsbeziehungen Japans. Institute for Development Policy (IFEP) Discussion Paper No. 11, August 1986

Harada, T./ The "softnomization" of Japan - A new concept
Pascha, W. to analyse economic development, in: ASIEN, No. 24, July 1987

5.2 Other Publications

Against the backdrop of existing contacts a great number of individual studies have emerged. The Japanese have examined problems of the German economy in various articles such as in "Characteristics of Agriculture and Agro-Policy in the Federal Republic of Germany" by M. Tokiwa (appeared in the economic journal of Keio University).

Furthermore, theoretical papers such as "Max Weber und die sozialwissenschaftliche Methodologie in der Gegenwart. Zum Verständnis der heutigen Bedeutung und Grenzen der Methodologie von Max Weber", by M. Kaneko have also been submitted (Institute for Development Policy (IFEP) Discussion Paper No. 4, 1983; appeared also in Japanese in the economic journal of Meiji University).

Japan has shown interest in the authors of the Freiburg Economics Faculty, and various book publications have appeared in Japanese translations:

Müller, J. H.   Methoden zur regionalen Analyse und Prognose, Tokyo

Müller, J. H.   Produktionstheorie

Schmidt, R.-B.   Wirtschaftslehre   der   Unternehmung,
                        Band I, Grundlagen und Zielsetzung,
                        Tokyo 1974

Schmidt, R.-B.   Wirtschaftslehre   der   Unternehmung,
                        Band II, Zielerreichung, Tokyo 1978

Schmidt, R.-B.   Wirtschaftslehre   der   Unternehmung,
                        Band III, Erfolgsverwendung (in print)

5.3 Planned Publications

- Harada, T.: Politische Ökonomie des Idealismus und der
  Romantik - Korporatismus von Fichte, Müller und Hegel

- Results of the Joint Seminar 1986 (Topic: The Role of
  Japan and the Federal Republic of Germany in the World
  Economy - with Special Reference to Small and Medium-
  Sized Companies)

- Results of the Joint Seminar 1988 (Topic: Protectionism
  vs. Liberalization)

VERKEHRSWISSENSCHAFTLICHE FORSCHUNGEN

Herausgegeben von Fritz Voigt

Seit 1975 sind erschienen:

DUNCKER & HUMBLOT / BERLIN

Schriften zu Regional- und Verkehrsproblemen in Industrie- und Entwicklungsländern

Herausgegeben von J. Heinz Müller und Theodor Dams

Seit Herbst 1972 sind erschienen: